The Abyssinia Crisis Seventy Years On

C000149433

Socialist History 28

Rivers Oram Press
London, Sydney and Chicago

Editorial Enquiries: Kevin Morgan, School of Social Sciences, University of Manchester, Manchester M13 9PL or kevin.morgan@manchester.ac.uk.

Reviews Enquiries: John Callaghan, School of Humanities, Languages and Social Sciences, University of Wolverhampton, Wulfruna Street, Wolverhampton WV1 1PB or j.callaghan@wlv.ac.uk

Socialist History 28 was edited by Allison Drew, Kevin Morgan, Andy Croft, David Howell and John Callaghan

Published in 2006
by Rivers Oram Press, an imprint of Rivers Oram Publishers Ltd
144 Hemingford Road, London, N1 1DE

Distributed in the USA by
Independent Publishers Group, Franklin Street, Chicago, IL 60610
Distributed in Australia and New Zealand by
UNIReps, University of New South Wales, Sydney, NSW 2052

Set in Garamond by NJ Design
and printed in Great Britain by T.J. International Ltd, Padstow

British Library Cataloguing in Publication Data
A catalogue record for this publication is available from the British Library
ISBN 1 85489 161 8 (pb)
ISSN 0969 4331

Contents

Dave Harker, *Tressell: The Real Story of the Ragged Trousered Philanthropists* (Andy Croft)

Norman LaPorte, *The German Communist Party in Saxony, 1924–1933: Factionalism, Fratricide and Political Failure* (Reiner Tosstorff)

William J. Fishman, *East End Jewish Radicals 1875–1914;* Rudolf Rocker, *The London Years* (Ben Birnbaum)

Peter Scholliers and Leonard Schwarz: *Experiencing Wages: Social and Cultural Aspects of Wage Forms in Europe Since 1500* (Jörn Janssen)

Joe England, *The Wales TUC 1974–2004: Devolution and Industrial Politics* (Keith Gildart)

Francis Beckett, *Stalin's British Victims* (Andrew Thorpe)

Ed Cray, *Ramblin' Man: The Life and Times of Woody Guthrie* (Ben Harker)

Moshe Lewin, *The Soviet Century* (John Callaghan)

Notes on Contributors

Gidon Cohen teaches at the University of Durham and is currently directing an ESRC-funded project on Labour Party activism. A revised version of his doctoral thesis on the ILP is to be published in 2006.

Allison Drew teaches African politics at the University of York. She is interested in anti-colonial and liberation movements.

Andrew Flinn teaches at University College, London, and with Matthew Worley edited *Socialist History 26* on youth cultures and politics.

Christian Hogsbjerg is writing a doctoral thesis on C.L.R. James in Britain.

David Howell teaches politics at the University of York. He edits the *Dictionary of Labour Biography* and has published widely on the British left and labour movement.

Willie Thompson is a former editor of *Socialist History* and a member of our editorial board. His most recent book is *Postmodernism and History*.

Margarita Tupitsyn is a scholar, critic, and curator. She is the author of books, catalogues, and numerous essays on twentieth century Russian and Soviet art. She is currently preparing an exhibition and catalogue entitled 'Against Kandinsky'.

Editorial

The year 2005 marks the seventieth anniversary of Italy's invasion of Ethiopia—final humiliating step in Europe's colonisation of Africa; bloody symptom of the collapse of collective security in Europe; harbinger of the world war to come. For millions in Africa and around the world Ethiopia—then called Abyssinia—was a potent symbol of African culture and resistance to colonisation. The state in Abyssinia traced its historical roots back to the first century AD and had adopted the Coptic Christian church in the fourth century AD. At the end of the nineteenth century it was ruled by a modernising monarchy whose expansionist aims collided with Italy's imperial ambitions during the years of European colonial conquest.[1]

In an attempt to regulate their competition for land and raw materials—the scramble for Africa that was risking to escalate into a European war—European political leaders assembled at the Berlin West African conference in 1884–5 to partition the African continent among themselves. The British and French empires claimed the lion's share of the continent. Italy, a lesser power, tried its luck, gaining control of part of Somaliland in 1888–9 and of territory along the southern Red Sea coast—modern-day Eritrea—in 1891. But when 17,000 Italian troops invaded Abyssinia in 1896, they suffered a crushing and humiliating defeat at the battle of Adwa.

Abyssinia's victory at Adwa thrilled Africa and the black world. But for Europeans, the Italian defeat became a challenge to step up their activities in the Horn of Africa. Italy, not content with its loss, extended its control over Somalia, established a settler colony in Eritrea and in 1911–12 conquered Libya. At the southern tip of the continent Cecil Rhodes plotted to gain control of the gold-bearing Transvaal in the name of the British empire. By the turn of the century most of Africa had been carved up amongst the rival European powers. Over the next decades, they extended their control from the coastlines to the interior, suppressing peasants, co-opting or banishing chiefs, conscripting labour to build railways connecting internal points of production with ports to facilitate the export of commodities to European markets.[2]

While Europe tightened its grip on Africa, fascism was sweeping across two European states. In Italy, Benito Mussolini came to power in 1922; in Germany Adolf Hitler took control in 1933. Willie Thompson's article on the Italian conquest of Abyssinia challenges a conventional wisdom that Italian fascism was not marked by the racism for which the Nazi regime is notorious. The stark brutality with which Italian troops slaughtered the Abyssinian people explodes that myth.

As tensions amongst European powers mounted in the early 1930s, Mussolini tried various diplomatic manoeuvres to gain control of Abyssinia —to no avail. The threats of invasion intensified. There was growing concern about the possibility of an assault on an independent and internationally-recognised state. The League of Nations had been formed in 1919 in the wake of the First World War to handle just such occurrences. Its covenant stipulated the protection of its members against external threats and authorised the use of economic and military sanctions. Abyssinia had been a member since 1923. Its emperor, Haile Selassie, appealed to the League for assistance in January 1935 and again in March.[3]

The League of Nations began its deliberations. Alongside its talks about sanctions, the working-class movement devised its own: in countries around the world, workers withdrew their own labour to hinder Italy's preparations for war. At the other end of the African continent news of Abyssinia's struggle electrified South Africans. 'It was the only political event that had roused the Africans for many years', wrote Eddie Roux, an early South African Communist. 'Many realised for the first time that there existed still in Africa an independent country where the black man was master and had his own king. They were inspired by the idea of black men defending their country against white aggressors.' When Italian agents in South Africa tried to organise the shipment of food supplies for their troops in East Africa their efforts backfired. From June through August 1935 dockworkers in Durban and Cape Town refused to load goods on Italian ships. 'Refuse to Ship Goods to Abyssinia! Defend the Last Independent Native State in Africa from the Attacks of Italian Imperialism!', appealed the Communist Party of South Africa.[4]

Mass protests took place across Africa. In South Africa the League against Fascism and War took a lead; a Friends of Abyssinia committee was launched in September 1935. The events gave a shot in the arm to the tiny South African left. Sales of the Communist Party organ, *Umsebenzi*, shot up to 7,000 a week, and the *African Defender*, organ of the local International Red Aid sold out at 10,000 an issue. A tiny Trotskyist group reported in October 1935 that its recent 'open air meetings broke all records. Last week, over a thousand workers listened to our views on the Italian-Abyssinian war, and this week nearly two thousand workers were present.'[5]

In British West Africa the solidarity movement for Abyssinia inspired the growth of African nationalist and Pan-Africanist sentiments. A generation of students and political activists—Namdi Azikwe and Duse Mohamed Ali in Nigeria and I. T. D. Wallace-Johnson in the Gold Coast, amongst others —organised protest meetings; Wallace-Johnson launched an Ethiopian Defence Committee, one of many that sprang up around the world.[6]

The support was not purely practical, nor was it restricted to Africa. The political struggle fertilised intellectual and cultural work, which in turn sharpened views on the struggle. The Trinidadian intellectual C. L. R. James was in England in the 1930s. Christian Hogsbjerg's article explores the impact of the Abyssinian struggle on James's research and thinking as he wrote *The Black Jacobins*, his masterful study of the Haitian Revolution. The French and Haitian revolutions are intertwined in James's account, just as the struggle in Abyssinia was interwoven with the politics and fate of Europe.

Despite the swell of popular support for the beleaguered country, the sanctions campaign was slow and controversial. Italy stepped up its aggression. Italian planes rained bombs on Adwa and Adigrat on 3 October 1935; its troops entered the country through Eritrea. Again Abyssinia appealed to the League, which finally imposed economic sanctions against Italy on 18 November. But the sanctions were limited—coal and oil were excluded—and were only as effective as its members' support. The United States had never joined the League and now failed to support the boycott, as did Germany. The Soviet Union supplied Italy with necessary materials during the war. Italy was able to stockpile its needed supplies. Britain, fearful of Mussolini's threat of a European war, allowed Italian ships to carry supplies and reinforcements for their army through the Suez Canal.[7]

When the League was first formed, economic and military sanctions had been seen as complementary weapons. Over time, however, they became interpreted as distinct choices, 'the difference being', explained political analyst E. H. Carr, 'that "economic sanctions" were obligatory and "military sanctions" optional'.[8]

The League's impotence in the face of Italy's aggression shattered any belief in its future use as a means to assure collective security. In December 1935 British foreign secretary Sir Samuel Hoare and French premier Pierre Laval proposed to concede most of Abyssinia to Mussolini in exchange for an end to the war. The plan provoked a public outcry; amidst accusations that they were betraying Abyssinia, the two politicians were forced to resign.

Yet their governments had no alternative policy to put in place. Appeasement became the order of the day.

For historian Arnold Toynbee the episode signalled the inherent 'covetousness' and 'cowardice' of human nature. For Carr, 'the bitter lesson of 1935–36 was needed to drive home the truth that in sanctions, as in war, the only motto is "all or nothing", and that economic power is impotent if the military weapon is not held in readiness to support it'. Power, concluded Carr, was 'indivisible'.[9]

The League's failure to stop the invasion did not mean that international support for Abyssinia dimmed. But the popular constituencies concerned about Abyssinia—especially trade unionists and left-wing activists—were a minority in Britain and the rest of Europe. Their support for Abyssinia was not transformed into the political strength needed to stave off Italian aggression. As Andrew Flinn and Gidon Cohen demonstrate, the left-wing anti-war coalition that had developed in Britain after the war of 1914–18 had not faced any serious challenge until the 1930s. Like the anti-militarist stance of the European powers in the League of Nations, Britain's anti-war alliance finally broke down over the Abyssinian crisis. The brutal events of the 1930s forced a redefinition of what it meant to be anti-war. They also exposed the impotence of the British left: while Mussolini's troops were killing Abyssinians, the Independent Labour Party, for one, was debating its principles and consulting its members on what it should have done to stop the invasion.

But if the British left, however ineffective, was concerned about Abyssinia, David Howell's discussion of the British general election of 1935 indicates that the British public showed far less interest, even though the crisis figured prominently in the electoral campaign. Voter preferences that year turned primarily on how political parties addressed economic, community and cultural issues. For many British politicians the significance of the Abyssinia crisis was the concern about the feasibility of collective security and, within a European context, the need to recruit Italy as an ally against a resurgent Germany. They feared that discord over Abyssinia could lead to an alliance between Berlin and Rome, a prospect that was rapidly realised. If the main concern of Europeans was Europe, Africans could find little hope in a League of Nations dominated by European powers.

Mussolini's was a war of colonial conquest at its most brutal—aerial bombardment and mustard gas. This time Abyssinian troops were unable to hold off the invading forces. On 5 May 1936 Italian troops captured the capital of Addis Ababa. Sylvia Pankhurst, suffragette, socialist, anti-fascist, founded the *New Times and Ethiopia News* that same month; 'at a moment when the fortunes of Ethiopia seem at their lowest ebb', she wrote, 'the greater then the need for an advocate and friend'. The paper exposed the brutal tactics and massacres used against the Abyssinians and went on to draw parallels with the unfolding war against fascism in Spain.[10]

While guerrilla struggles carried on inside the country, Haile Selassie went abroad in search of foreign assistance, appealing yet again to the League of Nations in June 1936. In vain—by 1937 Mussolini claimed victory over Abyssinia, a claim accepted by the outside world the following year. In Britain, the Chamberlain Government signed an Anglo-Italian Agreement on 16 April 1938, signalling its recognition of the Italian conquest.

The Italian occupation was a short-lived affair; five years later in 1941, during the Second World War that the League of Nations had failed to prevent, Ethiopia became the first African country freed from colonial rule. Its conquest had been the last step in the scramble for Africa; its struggle had inspired African nationalist and pan-African movements; its independence signalled, if then unrecognised, the coming end of the colonial era.[11]

Allison Drew

Notes

1. For background on Abyssinia see, inter alia, Christopher Clapham, *Haile-Selassie's Government* (London, 1969); David Buxton, *The Abyssinians* (Southampton, 1970); Edmond J. Keller, *Revolutionary Ethiopia: From empire to people's republic* (Bloomington and Indianapolis, 1991).
2. Basil Davidson, *Modern Africa* (London and New York, 1989 edn), pp.5, 60–1, 81–2; Roland Oliver, *The African Experience* (London, 1993), pp.176–8.
3. Alberto Sbacchi, *Ethiopia under Mussolini: Fascism and the Colonial Experience* (London: Zed, 1985); Denis Mack Smith, *Modern Italy* (New Haven and London, 1997), pp.385–6.
4. Edward Roux, *Time Longer than Rope: The Black Man's Struggle for Freedom in South Africa* (Madison, WI, 1964), pp.302–3; *Umsebenzi*, 22 June 1935.
5. Roux, *Time Longer than Rope*, pp. 302–3; extract of a letter of 24 October 1935 from the Communist League of South Africa, Press Service of the International Secretariat, International Communist League (B-L), 15 November 1935 in Allison Drew (ed.), *South Africa's Radical Tradition: A Document History*, vol.1, 1907–1950 (Cape Town, 1996), pp.157–8.
6. Davidson, *Modern Africa*, pp.78–9.
7. Sbacchi, *Ethiopia under Mussolini*, p.230; Mack Smith, *Modern Italy*, pp.386–7.
8. Edward Hallett Carr, *The Twenty Years' Crisis, 1919–1939* (New York, 1964), pp.28–9, 38–9, 118.
9. Carr, *Twenty Years' Crisis*, pp.39, 119.
10. Richard Pankhurst, 'Sylvia Pankhurst and Anti-Fascism', *Socialist History*, 19, (2001), pp.25–7.
11. Davidson, *Modern Africa*, p.61.

With this issue we are pleased to welcome the addition of a number of new editorial advisers, reflecting the international scope of interest that we hope the journal will continue to reflect. **John Saville**, of course, is already familiar to *SH* readers as contributor of the 'Books to be Remembered' series, as well as a former editor of *The Dictionary of Labour Biography* and *Socialist Register*, and author of a number of major historical works. **Donald Sassoon** will also be familiar to readers through the interview with him by Willie Thompson which appeared in *SH27*. Donald is author of the acclaimed *One Hundred Years of Socialism* (Deutscher Prize, 1997), and of a study (2001) of the reception of *Mona Lisa*. He has recently been working on a history of cultural production and consumption in Europe, forthcoming.

Both **Stuart Macintyre** and **Carlos Cunha** are known for their writings on communism. Stuart teaches history at the University of Melbourne and has written several books on both the British and Australian left, including *A Proletarian Science* (1980), *Little Moscows* (1980), and the first volume of a history of the Australian CP, *The Reds* (1998). His most recent book, *The History Wars* (2003), has stimulated wide debate as an account of the political contest over Australian history. Carlos, who teaches at Dowling College in New York State, is the author of *The Portuguese Communist Party's Strategy for Power, 1921–1986* (1992) and numerous other works on Portuguese politics.

Gregory Kealey is a Fellow of the Royal Society of Canada and will be known to readers as the founding editor of the Canadian labour history journal, *Labour/Le Travail*. His books include *Canadian History* (1995) and he has been working most recently on a study of *State Repression of Labour and the Left in Canada, 1914–1922*. **Lungisile Ntsebeza**, who teaches sociology at the University of Cape Town, is a South African political activist who in 1976 was arrested for his work in a small political group concerned with marxist ideas and their relevance in the South African liberation struggle. He was detained for eighteen months and sentenced to four years' imprisonment. His current research concerns democratisation in rural areas, and his book, *Democracy Compromised: Chiefs and the Politics of Land in South Africa*, is to be published shortly. **Boris Kagarlitsky** is a journalist, political and trade-union activist, and director of the Institute of Globalisation Studies, Moscow. His books in English include *The Thinking Reed* (1988) and *Farewell Perestroika* (1990). We are delighted to welcome them as editorial advisers, along with our new editorial board members, **Dianne Kirby** and **Kevin McDermott**.

Socialist History Titles

Requests for back issues to ro@riversoram.com

Previous issues of *Socialist History* include:

The Fascist Regime and the Abyssinia Crisis

Willie Thompson

There is a perception, particularly marked among sections of the Italian public and academic world, but also prevalent in other countries, that Italian
fascism was less barbarous in character than its German counterpart—compare the amount of television attention devoted to their respective
criminality—and that racism did not play a significant part in its ideological
formation. Neither supposition is entirely accurate.

In overall terms, the first one may be justified. Yet in their respective
struggles for power, Mussolini's *squadristi* between 1920 and 1922 were even
more violent and murderous than Hitler's Brownshirts during the crisis of
the Weimar Republic from 1929 until Hitler's establishment of the dictatorship in the summer of 1933. Nor, during their respective periods of
rule—before world war provided the Nazis with the opportunity to indulge
their exterminatory fantasies against Jews and other 'subhumans'—was
there all that much to choose between the regimes so far as oppressive
tyranny was concerned.[1]

In relation to the second, there is hardly any truth at all. Certainly it is true
that Italian fascism was much less disfigured by antisemitism than was the
case with Nazism—the fascist party even had some Jewish members and at
least one was murdered by the SS for this reason. As with some other fascist or quasi-fascist movements in the Mediterranean area—Spain and
Portugal for example—this particular form of racism was generally less in
evidence. Different historical, social and cultural traditions were involved.
In Italy the Jewish community was very small, 'uniquely integrated', and antisemitism had never been a significant issue.[2] It seems likely that this more
than anything else has been responsible for the milder attitude among sections of the Italian public towards Mussolini's dictatorship in comparison
with that north of the Alps. Italian fascists can be made to appear innocent
of any responsibility for the Holocaust.[3] 'Many historians see the race issue
as a qualitative mark of distinction between Fascism and Nazism', writes

Philip Morgan.[4] Consequently, while contemporary German neo-Nazism possesses a significant constituency, it is a marginalised one, and no respectable politician or public figure would have anything to do with it. In Italy today by contrast, neofascists sit in the government, Mussolini's grand-daughter, his unapologetic admirer, gets elected to the Italian parliament, and the definitive (at least in size) biography of the dictator, published in eight volumes by the late Renzo De Felice (*d.* 1996) is sympathetic and apologetic if not celebratory in tone.

However, when it came to racism in the broader sense of relations with people of colour, of conviction of Europe's inherent superiority and of contempt for the lives and property of people known as non-Europeans, of preparedness to treat them as expendable instruments, fascist attitudes were as ferocious as could be imagined. Similar outlooks were characteristic of all colonial regimes, but to the everyday racism typically prevalent in such situations was added in the fascist case a glorification of brutality, an obsession with ruling by fear, of responding to every hint of real or imagined resistance with sadistic and generalised terror. Such responses were personally encouraged and indeed insisted upon by Mussolini himself.

Italian fascism itself was a fairly incoherent ensemble of attitudes and values derived from different sources, among these an orientation towards imperialist ultra-nationalism. Its Abyssinian adventure has to be understood in that context, and a sketch of this background will put it in better perspective. As Denis Mack Smith observes,

> fascism was a party not of ideas and doctrine but of action. [Mussolini's] followers were a gang of truculent and ambitious men who wanted power, and were backed by some intelligent and influential members of society who saw the usefulness of such rowdies in helping to suppress socialism, curtail parliamentary liberties, and if possible make the name of Italy feared abroad.[5]

The above comment is taken from Mack Smith's book *Mussolini's Roman Empire*, which specifically addresses the empire-building aspect of the regime. Mack Smith is the doyen of historians writing in English on Italy in general and Italian fascism in particular, the most renowned contestant of Renzo De Felice's sympathetic interpretation.[6] *Mussolini's Roman Empire* demonstrates in detail that when it came to the conquest and occupation of Abyssinia, the fascist empire conceded nothing in atrocity and repression to the Nazi occupiers of Eastern Europe.

The imperialist background

Prior to the First World War the Italian state, only unified in 1871, is perhaps best described as an oligarchic liberal monarchy—liberal in the sense of the free market, a constitution, rule of law (after a fashion) and the existence of competing parties, including the Italian Socialist Party (PSI). But it was emphatically not democratic; real power rested exclusively with the elites (principally the northern ones) and the electorate, until 1913, remained tiny.[7] Linguistically, geographically and socially the state was poorly articulated; the economy, rather like the Russian, was generally backward with a few islands of advanced technological production.

Yet this inadequately situated ruling elite had ambitions far above its station. It wanted Italy to be a great power. In the late nineteenth century this meant a colonial policy—every respectable maritime great power (and even some not-so-great) had their complement of coloured bits on the world map. Italy however was a latecomer, achieving only a couple of not very choice colonies, Eritrea and Somalia, on the Horn of Africa, while an attempt to annex Abyssinia in 1896 turned into military catastrophe—leaving that feudal state virtually the only independent African entity on the continent and bitterly offending Italian nationalist sentiment.[8]

In 1910, at a time when Mussolini was still presenting himself as a firebreathing socialist, Enrico Corradini established the Italian Nationalist Association (ANI), later the Italian Nationalist Party (PNI) and subsequently absorbed by the fascists. The ANI linked domestic to foreign and colonial policy, demanding an authoritarian regime of efficiency and directed development as a suitable foundation for an aggressive colonial and foreign policy. In 1912 they got the aggression they wanted, when what is now Libya was wrested from the nominal control of the decrepit Turkish sultanate and formally added to the Italian empire—though in this case too, control was largely nominal.[9]

The Italian state's entry into the First World War, delayed until 1915, was more brazenly imperialist even than that of the other major combatants—the aim was to annex and dominate large territories on the eastern shore of the Adriatic as an initial stage towards control of the Mediterranean. The non-fulfilment of these aims and the notion of 'mutilated victory' contributed to the intensity of the anger among the nationalist middle classes that helped to propel Mussolini into power in 1922. The elements who most feared socialism, peasant insubordination and social disorder generally were the same ones who coveted great power status and plenty of overseas possessions:

An alternative to parliamentary government had been seriously proposed [already in 1900]; a strong executive, above corruption and the law, to suppress unrest at home and assert Italy's interests abroad. Later this was the Fascist program in outline. Indeed the fascists were to offer much of what the traditional Italian Right had failed to accomplish in 1900.[10]

Fascist victory was made possible by the support of the landed, industrial, commercial and military elites, together with the readiness of the *squadristi* to employ unconstrained violence with a ferocity that disorientated and demoralised their enemies. The same characteristics were to be evident thereafter in the pursuit of Italian colonial policy.

Even before Mussolini's elevation to the premiership and the institution of the full-blown dictatorship two years later, the ambitious governor of Libya 'who had already shown skill and ruthlessness in building up a huge financial empire in the Balkans',[11] had set about the effective reconquest of the colony. The regime, with Mussolini in the forefront, gave him and his military successors (the same generals soon to be delegated to overrun Abyssinia) every support, and in a ten-year war during which the Italian forces (including conscripts from the African colonies) demonstrated exceptional savagery, including the use of mass executions, sacking of population centres, concentration camps and starvation, the Libyans were ultimately ground down.[12] After this Mussolini (by this time at odds with Britain) took it upon himself to present himself as 'the defender of Islam' and, sitting astride a horse, waved a 'sword of Islam' (forged in Florence) that he had made an Arab delegation present him with.

Part of the propaganda surrounding this imperialist venture from the time of Libya's first seizure to its eventual subjugation twenty years later was that it would, under Italian management, prove a marvellous economic asset. Agricultural immigrants would be attracted there, so relieving overpopulation in the Italian countryside and raising its economic level. Libya would be turned into a granary as north Africa had been in Roman times, making Italy self-sufficient in grain and at the same time stimulating trade and shipping between the two countries. Needless to say, none of this had much basis in reality. Few Italians were willing to commit themselves to a future life in Libya.[13] While a number of individuals with the necessary connections in high places made large fortunes out of confiscated Arab land and property— 'fascist colonisation was associated with scandalous profits made by contractors and even by army officers'—as far as national revenue was concerned Libya was more of a liability than an asset.[14]

The Abyssinian context

All of these features, on an exaggerated scale, were present in the build-up to and the eventual assault upon Abyssinia in October 1935. The fascist regime had inherited from the Liberal state a lengthy and infamous tradition of imperial adventurism and to this had added its own blend of vindictive brutality, bombast, openly asserted longing to inspire terror and thirst for propaganda triumph. In addition there were new material considerations present in 1935.

The first of these was the evident one that with the Senussi insurgents in Libya finally subdued, the troops that had been used there were now available for deployment elsewhere—a military commander was named in early 1932 and an outline plan for invasion was ready later in the year.[15] Thus, Abyssinia can be viewed as no isolated undertaking but as part of a continuous process of territorial aggression beginning in the early days of the regime, carrying on later with Albania and Greece and culminating in the hope of still larger seizures in Europe in the role of Hitler's vassal. However, even more significant considerations were the impact of the great slump and consequent developments in central Europe.

The slump, triggered by the collapse of the New York stock exchange in October 1929, affected Italy severely, the more so as Mussolini had just insisted on the revaluation of the currency, designated with the usual fascist bombast as 'the battle for the lira'. This, with officially imposed wage reductions, had reduced domestic purchasing power and intensified the effects of the slump by making life even more difficult for Italian exporters and their workforces. Devaluation—which was being used everywhere else—would have helped. But this was unthinkable because it was seen as detrimental to fascist prestige. The distress of collapsed agricultural prices and rocketing industrial unemployment was added to the existing social distress. Even the advantage of falling consumer prices was denied to the workforce, with more government wage cuts between 1930 and 1934.[16] Other measures included the state rescue of the threatened banking system and encouragement of cartelisation, reinforcing the position of big capital.

Not even Mussolini however could be unaware that a crisis of such dimensions threatened any government seen to be presiding over it. In typical fascist style, the economic measures noted above were secondary to those of control and propaganda, in which territorial expansionism occupied a central place. For a start, the slump was presented as the crisis of liberal plutocracies, not of capitalism as such, and an indication that fascist standards would soon be adopted throughout Europe and more widely. The emergence or strengthening, consequent upon the slump, of fascist movements and organisations in other states was naturally presented in the same light.[17] Mussolini even made a gesture towards founding a fascist international, declaring in 1934 that 'between 1929 and the present day fascism has developed from a purely Italian phenomenon to become a universal phenomenon'.[18] Under the command of the National Fascist Party (PNF) secretary Achille Starache, who boasted he never did anything except on Mussolini's explicit instructions, supplementary organisations with quasi-compulsory or compulsory membership, were strengthened or multiplied in the attempt to create to a thoroughly totalitarian society ruled by the slogan 'Believe, Obey, Fight'.[19]

Within this context, even though there is no evidence that the regime was then under any imminent threat, the intended conquest of a new empire could be expected to have a considerable propaganda value, a classic diversionary tactic in cases of domestic trouble practiced by many governments from the nineteenth century onwards. In addition there would be immediate concrete benefits to the armament and associated industries and to employment within them. Nevertheless it was one thing to complete the subjugation of Libya, where Italian possession and sovereignty was internationally recognised, quite another to attack without provocation an internationally recognised state and member of the League of Nations such as Abyssinia.

Mussolini liked to brag that he was prepared to take on the whole world if necessary; such was the awe that he and his regime allegedly inspired. But he was perfectly capable of recognising that European circumstances would have to be propitious before he could risk embarking on such a venture. The price of failure could be very high and would be made the more likely if he faced all the principal European powers united in opposition.

Hitler's appointment as German chancellor at the beginning of 1933 changed all that. But it must not be assumed that because both dictators were fascists and Hitler praised Mussolini as his mentor that they necessarily saw eye to eye on all matters, particularly in regard to foreign policy. On the contrary, Hitler's clear ambition from the very outset to smash the Versailles treaty and redraw the European map, though it might ultimately provide a cover for Italian expansionist aims, represented a more immediate danger. For the reunification of Austria with Germany, listed as a priority in *Mein Kampf*, could only clash with Mussolini's self-appointed role as the protector of the Austrian clerico-fascist regime and his ambitions for Italian hegemony over its neighbouring states. Indeed, in 1934 the Duce moved troops to the Austrian frontier to discourage a putative Nazi takeover; added Italy's name to protests against German unilateral rearmament; signed an alliance with France and in 1935 even hosted a meeting of western powers unmistakably aimed against Germany (the Stresa Front). A suspicious stance towards the Reich was certainly the preference of the Italian diplomatic service at this time.[20]

Even at this stage, however, the establishment of the Nazi regime and its aggressive postures presented invaluable advantages so far as the planned attack on Abyssinia was concerned. First, by the creation of tension, disorder and fear on the diplomatic scene it promised to distract attention from Mussolini's moves in East Africa; second, if the new Germany was perceived as a potential threat to the western powers, that fact could make them willing to buy Italian support against it by looking the other way while he dismembered Haile Selassie's empire. This was indeed the deal Mussolini thought he had informally obtained when the representatives of the two countries avoided mentioning Abyssinia during the Stresa meeting, at a time when military preparations were well under way.[21]

In the event Germany's usefulness proved to be of a different sort. Mussolini may not have deceived himself when he expected that the French and British governments after a few mild and formal protests would wash their hands of his victim, for the Hoare-Laval agreement between the British and French foreign ministers in December 1935 offered the emperor surrender covered by a face-saving formula, whereby he would have ceded half his kingdom directly to Mussolini and become the latter's vassal for what remained. Mack Smith suggests that Mussolini would have been willing to accept this discreditable proposal.[22] But the diplomats had reckoned without the strength of public reaction in Britain and France, which responded with fury and forced the resignation of both appeasers.

Prior to this the League of Nations had unanimously condemned the aggression—it was so blatant and unaccompanied even by a declaration of war that the members could scarcely do otherwise. Under the League Covenant aggressors were required to be punished by the imposition of sanctions.[23] But the half-hearted attempt at sanctions proved worse than useless. In the first place, the sanctions did not include oil, the one commodity that would have made an impact, nor was any attempt made to deny Italy shipping passage through the Suez Canal. In the second place, the initial reaction in Italy to the beginning of hostilities had been muted, in spite of Starace's best efforts to organise spontaneous enthusiasm in October. As Mack Smith notes:

> Public opinion was not enthusiastic...According to police reports the bureaucracy, the aristocracy, and the leaders of the armed services were against the war, and in cinemas there was sometimes a dead silence as news reels were shown, or whistles of derision.[24]

Sanctions, however, mild and ineffective as they were, provided the opportunity for the fascist propaganda machine to present Italy as the victim of the selfish plutocratic powers aiming to deny Italy the colonies they themselves possessed in quantity. This achieved the objective of generating the widespread public support that had previously been lacking—for example large numbers of wedding rings were offered to help fund the invasion. According to Mussolini the sanctions 'broke the last resistance to Fascism in Italy'.[25]

It was in these circumstances that Italy's fateful shift from playing off Germany against the western powers towards the formation of the fascist axis occurred. Hitler provided Italy with arms and material (particularly coal) covered by the sanctions, and publicly supported the Italian position. He also thoughtfully supplied arms to the Abyssinians, hoping to prolong the war and so make Mussolini more dependent upon Germany and enable German industrialists to capture Italian markets in eastern Europe. He was rewarded by the growing conviction on Mussolini's part that his future—and future territorial profit—now lay in closer alignment with Hitler. By the beginning of 1936, encouraged by his more pro-Nazi sycophants, he was indicating that he was willing to accept German hegemony over Austria (if not yet unification).[26]

Character of the war

Meantime the war was progressing. The best-remembered aspect is that the Italian military used poison gas to attack the Abyssinian defenders.[27] Although Mussolini was later to claim that this was essential to ensure victory, that allegation was entirely bogus—the Italians had overwhelming conventional superiority—their main problem was the leadership's incompetence in deploying their assets. According to the veteran fascist Italo Balbo:

> rarely had an enterprise of such scope been staged with such a lack of skill or with such frivolous naiveté. The political, diplomatic, financial and, indeed, even military preparations had been completely inadequate.[28]

Mustard gas was only the beginning. The level of atrocity throughout the war—described, naturally, as a war of defence against a barbaric aggressor and the greatest colonial war in all history[29]—and following the proclaimed victory in May 1936 when Addis Ababa was occupied, was extravagant even by colonial standards. It was in Abyssinia, rather than in Spain, that the mass destruction of population centres by aerial bombardment was first pioneered. One of the invaders' first acts following occupation of the capital was to round up and slaughter every literate Abyssinian they could lay hands on, and to repeat this elsewhere in the country wherever they could. This was an act of deliberate policy specified by Mussolini, the aim being to destroy every element of the Abyssinian intelligentsia, for these, he reasoned, would provide the nuclei for any opposition and resistance that might arise against Italian rule. 'Haile Selassie later recalled', writes Mack Smith, 'that the first generation of Ethiopian elementary-school teachers was systematically exterminated and the development of the country consequently set back for decades.'[30] It was a policy that was applied with equal assiduousness by the Nazis three years later in Poland.

The capture of Addis Ababa was followed by the proclamation of the king of Italy as Emperor of Abyssinia. But this by no means meant that the war had concluded; most of the country remained outside Italian control, and in fact resistance continued well into 1937. However, the assertion that Abyssinia was now subject to Italian sovereignty meant that any resisters were declared to be rebels and immediately executed upon capture. Nor was that all. The use of poison gas continued, and for every Italian killed ten Abyssinians were executed at random, sometimes by burning them alive. This was accompanied by indiscriminate looting and massacre— estimated at thirty thousand dead in one episode after an attempted assassination of the viceroy Rudolfo Graziani—including execution of all adult males in villages where there was any suspicion of resistance.[31] One of the minor tropes in the propaganda barrage around the war was that the established religion in Abyssinia, the Christian Coptic church, was a schismatic breakaway from the true faith, and Italian conquest might produce the welcome result of leading the benighted natives back to Catholicism. Unsurprisingly then, the Coptic clergy were not spared in the general assault upon Abyssinian culture. On one occasion the entire personnel of a monastery, amounting to four hundred, were executed when arms were discovered on the premises.

In concrete terms the outcomes of the colonial war were wholly disadvantageous for the fascist regime. Mussolini had at one stage boasted that he would recruit three million Abyssinians as colonial soldiers, establish an armaments industry there to equip them (the country was imagined to be packed with the necessary raw materials), and so overrun the Sudan and possibly Egypt as well—or even carry Italian power across the continent to west Africa. That of course was pure fantasy—but so was the notion that conquered Abyssinia could attract millions of Italian settlers and become an invaluable economic asset to the metropolis. As was the case with Libya, few settlers were attracted—even fewer in fact—and the cost of the conquest and subsequent repression used up government financial reserves and created severe difficulties in this sphere.[32]

Diplomatically the position was no better. Internationally, the Duce had isolated himself. For future support he was now reliant exclusively on Nazi Germany, with all the implications of that situation. In return he had acquired a huge and rebellious imperial possession in east Africa located at the end of a long and fragile line of communication dominated by the state with which he had just fallen out and ruptured the understanding of the Stresa front. These developments were to have far-reaching consequences.

Yet, from Mussolini's point of view and in terms of the main aim of the aggression, which appears to have been more to demonstrate Italian power and ruthlessness to domestic and foreign audiences than to exploit territory and African populations, the plan had worked marvellously. All observers were agreed that after victory was announced, Mussolini had never been so popular or so widely acclaimed.[33] 'The Fascist system had apparently been validated by the achievement of empire.'[34] He purported to have successfully defied the decadent liberal states of western Europe—not to mention those who had followed their lead in the League of Nations—and courageously asserted the nation's military virility. Mussolini later remarked that he wished Italian deaths had been greater than the 1500 or so killed so that the enemy would have appeared more formidable.[35] The Italian public, of course, knew nothing of the incompetence that had characterised the military operations nor of the deliberate atrocities that had accompanied the campaign and subsequent Italian rule. Indeed they were told quite the opposite: that the Italian forces had conducted themselves with singular correctness and attention to humanitarian considerations, despite the regime's earlier portrayal of their victims as bestial illiterate savages, and that the Abyssinians were delighted to submit to their new masters.[36] It would not be too far from the truth to characterise the whole enterprise as a gigantic publicity stunt. Theatrical posturing backed by impudent lies was the stock in trade of the Italian fascist regime, and as always the tone was set by the Duce. His priority at all times was to give an impression of force, determination, invincibility and infallibility. As Mack Smith concludes:

> Mussolini, with his natural talent for propaganda, squeezed every possible advantage out of the victory, and managed to convince many people that it would bring jobs for everyone and admiration from the whole world …It was described as one of the great campaigns in world history, a masterpiece of strategy against an enemy which the military experts of Europe had guaranteed would be absolutely unbeatable.[37]

Consequences

A David Low cartoon at the time of the invasion showed Mussolini lifting a gigantic dustbin lid over a hole in the earth, from which a demon wreathed in flame and smoke is seen climbing. The caption read 'The man who took the lid off'. The cartoon proved prophetic.

As most commentators point out, the principal gains from the episode went to Hitler. He succeeded in turning a potential opponent and obstacle to his ambitions into an ally, and a dependent ally at that, thanks to the over-stretch Mussolini had indulged in. Mussolini knew it too. When Starhemberg visited Rome in spring 1936, he 'found the Duce preoccupied with the threat of German power and the way in which his own quarrel with Britain and France was working to Hitler's advantage'.[38] The Axis was now Italy's destiny. Rome had lost any further opportunity of diplomatic manoeuvring between Germany and the western powers. Hitler, by contrast, gained diplomatic elbow room with the burial of the Stresa front.

Hitler lost no time in seizing the moment. In March 1936, while London and Paris were still preoccupied with the ongoing war in Africa, German troops reoccupied the Rhineland, part of Germany, but demilitarised by the Versailles Treaty—a status reaffirmed by the Locarno Treaty of 1925, which Germany too had voluntarily signed. 'The opportunity was provided by Mussolini', argues Ian Kershaw.

> [The]Abyssinian adventure, provoking the League of Nations' condemnation of an unprovoked attack on a member-state and the imposition of economic sanctions, broke the fragile Stresa Front. Italy, faced with a pessimistic military outlook…and looking for friends, turned away from France and Britain and towards Germany…The path to the 'Axis' immediately opened up.[39]

The consequences of the Anglo-French failure to react to this breach were momentous. Hitler's domestic position was further secured; the move was enormously popular in Germany. His hold over his generals, who had been less than enthusiastic about the gamble, was correspondingly enhanced. At the same time, the French architecture of alliances in eastern Europe designed to curb German power (known as the Little Entente) was fatally undermined. The Poles, who had offered military assistance if France reacted, were left especially embarrassed. The Austrian regime, in a state of strained relations with Germany since an unsuccessful Nazi coup in 1934 and continuing underground Nazi interference in its affairs, began to mend its fences with Hitler (not that it was to do it any good in the long run). Mussolini had no option but to make the best of it.

In July of the same year, a military revolt by reactionary Spanish generals against the popular front government precipitated civil war. Partly out of ideological sympathy and also to strengthen his regime's position in the Mediterranean, Mussolini dispatched immediate assistance to the ultra-right forces. At first he imagined that a few Blackshirt volunteers would suffice, having reinforced his illusions of Italian invincibility by the Abyssinian 'success'. But he soon discovered that it would be necessary to commit substantial military forces to avoid political humiliation.

Hitler now judged the moment opportune to increase his solicitation of Mussolini for a closer partnership. He deployed the flattery to which the Duce was at all times susceptible, referring to him as 'the greatest statesman on earth, to whom no one else might even remotely compare himself', and assuring him that German expansionist aims were confined to northern and eastern Europe and that the Mediterranean was an exclusively Italian sphere as far as Germany was concerned.[40] Hitler was entirely successful; by October Mussolini was openly referring to a 'Rome-Berlin Axis'.

According to Mack Smith, Mussolini's triumph in Abyssinia and military intervention in Spain so superheated his aggressiveness and self-confidence that he gloried in the foreign hatred he was attracting and in the course of 1937 left the League of Nations, establishing a tripartite Anti-Comintern Pact with Germany and Japan.[41] He was planning further conquests, starting with Britain in Egypt—this supposedly 'shocked' his generals—but prudently decided to wait until he had finished off democracy in Spain.[42] His diplomatic hands were therefore tied to the extent that he had to accept the German annexation of Austria in March 1938 and see what had hitherto been the key pillar of his regime's foreign policy finally shattered. He consoled himself with the pretence that he was the world statesman who solved the Czech crisis at Munich in September. By this time the initiative was wholly in Hitler's hands—he was by now clearly the senior fascist dictator. By September 1939 the Duce was left with the alternatives of either joining Hitler as a subordinate ally or keeping Italy a bystander in the conflict—the position he had scorned and denounced in the First World War, thereby launching himself on the road to power. The Italian public, it might be added, despite the propaganda deluge powered upon them, showed no genuine enthusiasm for these developments. Traditionally its sentiments tended towards Britain and France however much it might have been affronted by the economic sanctions of previous years.

Abyssinia and Italian history

Among apologists—not all of them neofascists[43]—and semi-apologists for the Italian dictatorship, the distinction from Nazism, in particular the relatively low profile of racism prior to the institution of the Salò republic in September 1943, was crucial. Above all, the claimed exemption for responsibility for the Holocaust was claimed to set Italian fascism apart. 'If "Auschwitz" represented the ultimate degradation of the human spirit and made plain the final contradiction of modernity, then the Italians had no real part in it', remarks Richard Bosworth.[44]

Any understanding of the judgements made of Mussolini and the fascist regime in Italian historiography and public understanding has to begin with the structure of Italian politics in the years following the end of the Second World War. Italy was an anomaly in democratic western Europe. Aside from France, it was the only state possessing a large and widely supported communist party. Even more alarming for the Atlanticist consensus inside and outside Italy, in the early 1970s the Italian communists were, under their flexible and respected leadership, continuing to make advances; the French communists, by contrast, were in political retreat. The communist party in Italy was above all identified with anti-fascism and the wartime resistance, the principal reason why it had such a significant hold on the public consensus.

The mid-seventies saw the initiation of a paper war by writers whom Bosworth describes as 'anti-anti-fascists', which nonetheless concealed its political purposes under the guise of academic objectivity and fidelity to the archives, and to which De Felice and his school was central. Whether explicitly or implicitly, this writing tended to rehabilitate Mussolini and his regime, complaining, in the words of one critic of the anti-anti-fascists, that 'the Resistance destroyed Italian national identity and prevented its reconstruction'.[45] It is not surprising that the interview in which De Felice's position was unambiguously expressed (he was a very convoluted writer) was distributed free by the big business association, the *Confindustria*.[46]

It cannot be denied that the campaign was remarkably successful—it laid the cultural foundation for the present state of Italian politics.[47] But its foundations rested upon a gigantic falsehood—the dissociation of the Italian fascist regime from Hitlerism and its allegedly more moderate and modernising character. This perception was reinforced by a text that came from outside and not intended to be in any way apologetic—Jonathan Steinberg's *All or nothing: the Axis and the Holocaust*, which compares the respective dictatorships' conduct in the course of the war, with especial attention to the Balkans.[48]

However, the appropriate comparison is not with the somewhat

Eurocentric concentration on racial stereotyping and its consequence in Europe, but what went on in the 'relatively invisible' Italian empire, with Abyssinia as the prime example. The treatment of the Senussi in Libya was a precursor. In the early 1930s 'at least 100,000 Libyans' were expelled from their homes and starved to death in a concentration camp, 'victims of a policy defined by its historian "as possessing the nature and extent of an authentic genocide"'.[49] De Felice did not write much on the Italian overseas empire, but he went so far as to suggest that there had been 'too much moralising about Fascist policies in Africa and the rest of the Italian Empire'.[50] Most controversially, he concluded that the Abyssinian campaign represented 'Mussolini's political masterpiece'.[51]

The horrors visited upon the Abyssinians during the course of the war and in its aftermath fully exceeded—always excepting the antisemitic dimension—those of the Nazis in any of their western European conquests. For a comparison it is necessary to turn to those parts of eastern Europe where colonisation, enslavement and massive population movements were the order of the day. In east Africa as in eastern Europe, racist fury was the order of the day: more and worse would have been inflicted but for the notorious inefficiency of the Italian military and administrative machine in comparison with those of its partner. The slide towards public forgetting has been represented not only at the academic and directly political level. In spite of overwhelming documentary evidence, not until the mid-1990s did the ministries of defence and foreign affairs admit that the invaders had used poison gas, and they covered it up thereafter—though this 'small victory ran against the norm'.[52]

It should be emphasised that it is not only English-speaking historians such as Mack Smith and Bosworth who have struggled against the trend. Italian historians, too, have taken a similar stand. Most notable is Angelo Del Boca—who forced the poison gas admission from officialdom—in spite of the abuse and threats directed against him. In Italian contemporary politics Abyssinia remains a live issue because of the light it throws on the Mussolini years. It is not only because of the seventieth anniversary that it is worth revisiting.

Notes

1. Richard Bessel (ed.), *Fascist Italy and Nazi Germany: comparisons and contrasts* (Cambridge, 1996) discusses detailed comparisons in a range of areas.
2. Bessel, *Fascist Italy*, p.13.
3. During the war the Italian military protected Jews in the Italian-occupied area of southeast France and in similar areas of the Balkans. On the other hand, some very senior Fascists, including individuals close to Mussolini, were as antisemitic as any Nazi. R.J.B. Bosworth, *The Italian Dictatorship* (London, 1998), p.4 writes:

'The Salò Republic…forgot the banality of good and assisted its German allies in the killing of more than 7500 Jews who had been resident in Italy and its Empire'.

4. Philip Morgan, *Italian Fascism 1919–1945* (London, 1995), pp.160ff. for Mussolini's personal antisemitism and introduction of antisemitic decrees in 1938.

5. Denis Mack Smith, *Mussolini's Roman Empire* (Harmondsworth, 1977), p.1.

6. He is 'one of the most sought-after and widely known foreign commentators on Italian politics and affairs'—from the citation at the award in 2004 for career achievement of the Society for Italian Studies Annual Awards (New York), http://faculty.valenciacc.edu/ckillinger/sihs/AnnualAwards.htm.

7. The faction-ridden governing party during this period was termed the Liberal Party.

8. Liberia was also formally independent, but that too was a colony of a kind.

9. Mack Smith, *Mussolini's Roman Empire*, p.36.

10. Alan Cassels, *Fascist Italy* (London, 1969), p.9.

11. Cassels, *Fascist Italy*, p.9.

12. Cassels, *Fascist Italy*, pp.39–40

13. According to Mack Smith, *Mussolini's Roman Empire*, p.115, there were initially about 1500 families and later a further 1800.

14. Mack Smith, *Mussolini's Roman Empire*, p.115.

15. Denis Mack Smith, *Mussolini* (London, 1983), p.202. The military commander was Emilio De Bono, executed despite his great age on Mussolini's orders in the last days of his regime.

16. Philip Morgan, *Italian Fascism*, p.128, notes: 'The intrinsically Fascist character of the regime's economic crisis management was in the continued coercion of labour.'

17. Since the 1920s Mussolini had been supplying such groups with finance and encouragement in Austria, Hungary, Germany and Croatia. This increased after 1929 as the conditions for foreign fascist growth improved generally. In 1932 he subsidised Oswald Mosley in establishing the British Union of Fascists, a fairly exact copy of the Italian style.

18. Jerzy W. Borejsza, 'East European Perceptions of Italian Fascism', in Stein Ugelvik Larsen, *Who Were the Fascists?: Social Roots of European Fascism* (Oslo, 1980), p.362.

19. Such as the *Opera Nazionale Dopolavoro* (equivalent to the Nazi 'Strength through Joy'). This had existed since 1936, but now became more prominent. Unemployment relief, such as it was, was also handled through a PNF subsidiary. The word totalitarian was invented by Mussolini as a term of approval.

20. Mack Smith, *Mussolini's Roman Empire*, p.91.

21. Mack Smith, *Mussolini's Roman Empire*, p.66.

22. Mack Smith, *Mussolini's Roman Empire*, p.73.

23. These developments occurred prior to the Italian invasion. Abyssinia raised the issue in March and Britain proposed sanctions in September. In view of the Hoare-Laval Pact it can be concluded that the move was meant as a deterrence

rather than as a serious engagement with fascist aggression.

24. Mack Smith, *Mussolini's Roman Empire*, p.70.

25. Mack Smith, *Mussolini's Roman Empire*, p.71.

26. Mack Smith, *Mussolini's Roman Empire*, p.91.

27. Attempts were made to conceal the use of this weapon due to the international horror it evoked. Foreign correspondents soon exposed it, but Italians were never allowed to know that this had happened.

28. Mack Smith, *Mussolini*, p.231.

29. Mack Smith, *Mussolini*, pp.229, 223.

30. Mack Smith, *Mussolini's Roman Empire*, p.78.

31. Mack Smith, *Mussolini's Roman Empire*, p.80.

32. The Germans estimated that in 1940 there were only 854 agricultural settler families in the whole of Italian East Africa. Mack Smith, *Mussolini's Roman Empire*, p.109.

33. Tobias Abse, 'Italian Workers and Italian Fascism' in Bessell (ed.), *Fascist Italy and Nazi Germany*, pp.40–60.

34. Morgan, *Italian Fascism*, p.144.

35. Mack Smith, *Mussolini*, p.233.

36. To emphasise this distinction there was no declaration of war, and the League was condemned for putting uncivilised Africans on the same level as civilised Italians.

37. Mack Smith, *Mussolini's Roman Empire*, p.76.

38. Alan Bullock, *Hitler: A Study in Tyranny* (London, 1955), p.317.

39. Ian Kershaw, *Hitler: 1889–1936 Hubris* (London, 1998), p.583.

40. Mack Smith, *Mussolini*, p.241. Hitler had laid down in *Mein Kampf* alliance with Britain and Italy as a key element in German geopolitical strategy.

41. Formal alliance with Germany was delayed till May 1939, by which time Hitler had deprived him of all other options.

42. Mack Smith, *Mussolini*, p.247.

43. For example the American commentators A.J. Gregor and Michael Ledeen.

44. Bosworth, *Italian Dictatorship*, p.3.

45. Bosworth, *Italian Dictatorship*, p.35, quoting Claudio Pavone. Bosworth devotes much of his volume to this historiographical conflict and De Felice's role in it.

46. Bosworth, *Italian Dictatorship*, p.122.

47. Though the PCI was put on the defensive even more by the activities of the Red Brigades and the murder of Aldo Moro.

48. Jonathan Steinberg, *All or Nothing: the Axis and the Holocaust* (London, 1990). Steinberg is careful, however, to note Italian fascists' ferocity and cruelty in other situations.

49. Bosworth, *Italian Dictatorship*, p.4.

50. Bosworth, *Italian Dictatorship*, p.103.

51. Bosworth, *Italian Dictatorship*, p.3.

52. Bosworth, *Italian Dictatorship*, p.179.

C.L.R. James and Italy's Conquest of Abyssinia

Christian Hogsbjerg

'Ethiopia was the last piece of Africa left free. Mussolini decided that he wanted it. The League of Nations had sworn to defend it. Every Negro with a spark of pride knows what happened, and remembers it with justified bitterness.' So wrote the late Trinidadian intellectual C.L.R. James in 1939, damning the idea that black people should support a war against fascist 'aggression' waged by the 'democratic' US and British governments, 'the very men who actively collaborated with Mussolini in destroying the last independent African state'.[1] Fascist Italy's conquest of Ethiopia, or what was then Abyssinia, in 1935–6 provoked in James not just a feeling of 'justified bitterness' after the conflict, but outrage as Mussolini's war plans became clear in early 1935.

This article will look at James's political response to the war while he was resident in Britain, but also the way in which it was shaped by his prior independent historical studies into the Haitian revolution of 1791–1803. In 1938 James turned this research into the classic account of 'the only successful slave revolt in history', *The Black Jacobins: Toussaint L'Ouverture and the San Domingo Revolution*.[2] In a rare discussion of how James came to write this pioneering 'history from below', Stuart Hall argued that 'what is riveting…is the way in which the historical work and the foregrounded political events are part of a kind of seamless web. They reinforce one another.'[3] This article will try to elucidate a portion of this 'seamless web' by examining how Italy's invasion and occupation of Abyssinia, just one 'foregrounded political event', 'reinforced' James's understanding of the San Domingo revolution. However, for James, history was not just something to be written about, but something to be made, and the article will also try to demonstrate the extent to which James's developing interest in the San Domingo revolt helped reinforce his political response to Mussolini's barbarism.

James first became interested in the Haitian revolution while teaching English and history in Trinidad in the 1920s. This was largely the result of his commitment to the growing movement for Trinidadian self-government, which had led James to look deeper into the pioneers of West Indian nationalism, such as John Jacob Thomas. James discovered that Thomas was also a schoolmaster 'without European or university education of any kind'. Yet in 1889 Thomas wrote a work titled *Froudacity: West Indian fables explained*, which demolished a bigoted attack on the West Indian people's capacity for self-government, *The English in the West Indies* (1888), by the noted English academic James Anthony Froude.[4] James clearly felt inspired by Thomas's example. In the summer of 1931, James recalled that a 'distinguished scientist' at the Imperial College of Tropical Agriculture 'foolishly took it upon himself to write an article proving that Negroes were as a race inferior in intelligence to whites. I wasn't going to stand for that and in our little local magazine I tore him apart'.[5]

It was in this short article called 'The Intelligence of the Negro', published in *The Beacon*, that James first wrote about Toussaint L'Ouverture.[6] James now started 'reading everything' he could on the Haitian revolution, but he could find no books of 'serious historical value' while in Trinidad.[7] He had been particularly angered by reading one 'very bad' biography of L'Ouverture—Percy Waxman's *The Black Napoleon* (1931). James thought 'what the goddam hell is this?' 'I was tired of hearing that the West Indians were oppressed, that we were black and miserable, that we had been brought from Africa, and that we were living there and that we were being exploited.'[8] After travelling to England in 1932 to make his way as a writer, James recalled, 'I began to look for materials and found only the same shallow ones I had read in the Caribbean. I immediately began to import books from France which dealt seriously with this memorable event in French history.'[9]

However, despite his reading and studying, at this point James seems to have regarded this 'memorable' revolution as an inspiring event only in a general sense. That he felt it had little immediate relevance to the modern world can be seen from an article he wrote in 1933 on 'Slavery Today,' to mark the centenary of the passing of the act of parliament which officially abolished slavery in British colonies. In it, James passed over the struggles of the slaves themselves against bondage and was happy to give most of the credit for the abolition of slavery to British reformers, something he had no doubt been taught while a student at Queen's Royal College. He had been deeply impressed by a great-aunt who had once been a slave, and had 'often heard her speak of what slavery meant'. He described what her freedom meant to her, but did not mention the San Domingo revolt of 1791–1803 at all, even though it was undoubtedly central to securing that freedom. As he noted of the 1833 act of parliament, for West Indians, 'our history begins with it. It is the year One of our calendar. Before that we had no history.'

Nevertheless, James was very concerned by what he had discovered about the state of slavery in the modern world. He pointed out that in 1833 there were 700,000 slaves worldwide, but that, one hundred years on, 'the shackled who have no future' amounted to more than five million. The commercial trade in these black slaves still continued, and 'all civilised countries must bear their share of blame'; indeed 'there are still thousands of slaves within the British Empire'.[10] At this time James can perhaps be best described as a Fabian socialist.[11] He had joined the British Labour Party, and was on the executive of the moderate League of Coloured Peoples. His proposals for abolishing the slavery that still existed in 1933 were timid, to say the least. 'We must get our own house in order. We owe that at least to the memory of Wilberforce and the other pioneers whose work we are celebrating today', he wrote. James suggested that there was, fortunately, 'a weapon close to hand which can end the evil', a Permanent Commission on Slavery at the League of Nations and so 'pressure must be brought to bear on the League' by the British government. 'Public opinion, ten times more powerful now than in 1833, will do the rest.'[12]

Very soon, however, James was to radically alter his perspective on how slavery could be abolished in the modern world. Central to this was James's profound and rapid orientation towards Marxism, a political transition not uncommon at that time, given the economic, political and ideological crisis engulfing global capitalism during the Great Depression. Having spent most of 1932 in Lancashire, James witnessed the impact of the slump on the local cotton industry and also met class-conscious workers in the town of Nelson, a 'Little Moscow', where he initially stayed. James was particularly gripped by reading Leon Trotsky's *History of the Russian Revolution*, published in Britain in 1932–3, which introduced him to Marxist theory. His strong sense of fair play then led him to read Stalin, then Lenin and Marx 'in order to trace back the quarrel', as he would later put it. James independently arrived at a commitment to Trotsky's ideas, though they flew in the face of the prevailing left-wing intellectual fashion for orthodox communism.[13] In the summer of 1933, after moving down to London, his developing ideas were soon challenged when he ran into his long lost childhood friend Malcolm Nurse. Nurse had now become 'George Padmore', the legendary leading black figure in the Communist International (Comintern). Padmore was the head of the Profintern, the Red International of Labour Unions' (RILU) International Trade Union Committee of Negro Workers (ITUC-NW). He edited their paper, *Negro Worker*, and was the author of six pamphlets including *The Life and Struggles of Negro Toilers* (1931), which, like most things Padmore wrote, had been banned by colonial governments immediately.[14] James heard Padmore speak about the mass struggles of black people across the world, but particularly in Africa. James recalls he was entranced because the Labour Party, of which he was still officially a member, never seemed to hold any meetings on the colonial question, let alone 'the coming revolution' in Africa.[15]

Hearing Padmore speak must have opened James's mind up to the potential of African people themselves to win their freedom. He later recalled:

> there was an exhibition of African art in 1933, I think the first one that had been held in Britain...I went because it was African, and because it was art, something new. I was about thirty-two years old and for the first time I began to realise that the African, the black man, had a face of his own. Up to that time I had believed that the proper face was the Graeco-Roman face. If a black man had that type of face he had a good face, and if he didn't, well, poor fellow, that was his bad luck...I went to this exhibition, I bought the catalogue, I bought some books.[16]

James continued to educate himself politically through reading hard, while working as a cricket reporter for the *Manchester Guardian*. When the cricket season was over, James travelled to France to spend six months searching in the Paris archives for more material on the Haitian revolution.[17] There he found many more exhibitions on African and black culture. As a result, by 1934, he explained, 'I began to look at the West Indians whom I knew, look at people, and I began to see people in a way I had never seen them before'.[18] His reading of Marxism was also shaping the way he saw working-class people in general, but it was not until he witnessed a spontaneous general strike in Paris against the growing fascist threat in February 1934 that he finally decided to seek out and join the Trotskyist movement. On his return to Britain, where Oswald Mosley's British Union of Fascists was starting to take root, he eventually tracked down a tiny group of Trotskyists in London and threw himself into making propaganda for international socialism.[19]

The International African Friends of Abyssinia

Mussolini's war plans and intentions to invade the East African state of Abyssinia became clear in early 1935, and it was James's new found sense of black identity that spurred him to throw himself into organising solidarity with the Abyssinians. As Robert Weisbord has noted, 'perhaps no single event in the twentieth century more clearly illuminated the nexus between diaspora blacks and continental blacks than the Italian-Ethiopian war'. This was because of the collective memory of Abyssinia, with both 'an impressive cultural tradition traceable to ancient Axum and a uniquely successful resistance to the European intrusion in Africa in the latter part of the nineteenth century'.[20] Together with Liberia, Abyssinia was one of the last areas of Africa free from European control, having heroically defeated Italy at the battle of Aduwa in 1896. However, Italy, particularly under Mussolini's fascist regime, had never lost the desire to take revenge and claim Abyssinia as one of its colonial possessions. Since 1932, Italian troops had been preparing for this and, as both Italy and Abyssinia were members of the League of Nations, in January and March 1935, the East African state requested the League to act to stop the looming illegal war of aggression.[21]

Through the League of Coloured Peoples, James had met Amy Ashwood Garvey, the former wife of Marcus Garvey, the Jamaican born pan-Africanist and founder of the Back to Africa movement. Amy Ashwood Garvey and Marcus Garvey had been founding members of the Universal Negro Improvement Association.[22] Amy Ashwood Garvey now lived in London, and co-owned the Florence Mills Night Club, a 'haunt of black intellectuals'.[23] James remembered that they both 'felt that there ought to be an opposition' to Mussolini's war, and that Ashwood Garvey had 'a unique capacity to concentrate all the forces available and needed for the matter in hand'.[24] Together they revived an ad-hoc committee formed in 1934 to aid the Gold Coast Aborigines' Rights' Protection Society deputation to England, and united it with a former communist front group, the Council for Promoting Equality and Civil Rights between White and Coloured People.[25] James became chair of the resulting International African Friends of Abyssinia (IAFA).[26]

James was now faced with the need to reconcile his frantic political activity with his professional work, serenely reporting cricket for the *Manchester Guardian*. On Monday 29 July 1935, readers of the *Manchester Guardian* might have read James's report on the match between Hampshire and Lancashire at Southampton played the Saturday before. 'The dullness of the innings was enlivened by music from a loudspeaker, a brass band, singing, and periodical discharges from a gun'. While 'it sounded far more exciting than the cricket…the gunfire next door continued with no regard for the batsman's concentration', nearly leading one Lancashire batsman to be dismissed in an untimely fashion. James discovered that the gunfire came from the stadium adjacent, where 'the local Conservative party made demonstration', and so they had been interrupted from their cricket by what James called a 'political diversion'. 'Cricket', James noted wryly, 'should be kept well away from politics.' However, ten pages on, keen readers of that Monday's *Guardian* might have spotted a report of the launch meeting of the IAFA that took place the night before, Sunday 28 July, in Farringdon Memorial Hall, London. In that report, one 'C.L.R James', their beloved cricket reporter, apparently 'gave a lucid history of the European treaties with Abyssinia' and declared that 'Abyssinia is a symbol of all that Africa was and may be again, and we look on it with a jealous pride'.[27] Of course, by Monday, James himself was back in Southampton to report on the continuing match between Hampshire and Lancashire.[28]

In fact it seems that James had suffered from a 'cricket diversion' during that IAFA launch meeting. Possibly still thinking about Lancashire's batting, he remembered, 'I got myself into a blunder. Being a Marxist I was naturally opposed to the League of Nations, but in the excitement of forming the organisation we passed a resolution demanding...that the League of Nations take steps against the Italian Government.'[29] That such a proposal was passed is not surprising, given the faith that was put in 'collective security' not just within the Abyssinian government and British Labour Party, but among the wider British population. As James recalled, 'Lord Robert Cecil, a League of Nations maniac, instituted a private poll. It gathered over eleven million votes for collective security and over six million for an armed League of Nations.'[30] When the results of this 'Peace Ballot' were published in late June 1935, it showed that many people in Britain were deeply unhappy at the Tory-dominated National Government's foreign policy and the prospect of another war. In less than a month, pragmatically thinking of British colonial possessions in East Africa, the new prime minister Stanley Baldwin took the opportunity to dramatically steal the wind from Labour's sails, claiming that 'collective security' through the League was now 'the sheet-anchor of British policy'.[31] James noted 'there were certain political elements who were extremely glad that our organisation, which was pretty widely known among the limited circles who were interested in these matters, could be included among those who were urging the intervention of the League of Nations'.[32]

Yet it is doubtful whether either the National Government or Labour opposition would have been able to cite the IAFA as supporting their position for long. As James remembered:

> most of us who were in the organisation and who were supporting it, had a conception of politics very remote from debates and resolutions of the League. We wanted to form a military organisation which would go to fight with the Abyssinians against the Italians. I think I can say here with confidence that it would have been comparatively easy to organise a detachment of blacks in Britain to go to Ethiopia.[33]

Many black people felt that Abyssinia was, in the words of IAFA member Ras Makonnen, 'the black man's last citadel'. Makonnen recalled that 'letters simply poured into our office from blacks on three continents asking where they could register'.[34] On 1 August 1935, British foreign secretary Sir Samuel Hoare argued that if Italy invaded Abyssinia it would 'inevitably lead' to 'the formidable unsettlement of the great coloured races of the world'.[35] James's IAFA were determined to do their bit to prove him correct. Their attempt to form an 'International Brigade' to fight fascism created, James remembered, 'something of a political stir at the time'.[36] By their own account, the hopes of the IAFA were dashed by the Foreign Enlistment Act of 1870. This forbade British subjects to join forces of countries—in this case Italy and Ethiopia—which maintained friendly relations with Britain.[37]

That an established cricket journalist like James, who had no military experience, should be willing to consider fighting in Abyssinia requires additional explanation. Robin D. G. Kelley has argued that James, 'as a Black man who probably felt a tinge of pride in Ethiopia's legacy, and whose admiration for Africa ran much deeper than anti-imperialism…felt obligated to defend the place of his ancestors'.[38] There is undoubtedly something in this, as James indicated in the letter to his comrades in the Independent Labour Party (ILP) that was published on 3 June 1936 in the *New Leader*. He hoped to join the Abyssinian army to make contact with 'the masses of the Abyssinians and other Africans'. 'I did not intend to spend the rest of my life in Abyssinia, but, all things considered, I thought, and I still think, that two or three years there, given the fact that I am a Negro and am especially interested in the African revolution, was well worth the attempt.'[39]

However, the letter also gives an indication of how James's willingness to consider fighting in Abyssinia reflected in part his study of what he would later call the victorious Haitian 'revolution for national independence…a people's war'.[40] In the Abyssinian army, James felt, 'I would have had an invaluable opportunity of gaining actual military experience on the African field where one of the most savage battles between Capitalism and its opponents is going to be fought before very many years'. He reveals a keen sense of some of the strategy and tactics needed for victory, noting that 'I believed also that I could have been useful in helping to organise the anti-Fascist propaganda among the Italian troops'. He felt that an uncompromising national liberation struggle would be won through guerrilla war. 'As long as the Emperor was fighting Imperialism I would have done the best I could.' However, James also reflected that if the emperor surrendered, 'I would have identified myself with those bands, hundreds of thousands of them, who are still fighting, and for years are going to carry on the fight against Imperialistic domination of any kind'.[41]

Could James's research have inspired him to seriously consider the possibility that history could repeat itself, that the Abyssinians could humiliate the vastly more militarily powerful European forces as the slaves on San Domingo had? After all, the slaves in San Domingo had been 'two-thirds raw Africans from the Guinea Coast in a strange country, many of them not knowing the language'.[42] Yet the process of revolutionary war saw these 'half-a-million slaves...trembling in hundreds before a single white man' become transformed into 'a people able to organise themselves and defeat the most powerful European nations of their day'.[43] Abyssinia had a black population of six million, fully twelve times that of San Domingo, which included a slave population of 'upward of two million'. Moreover, unlike the slaves of San Domingo, these slaves were not strangers in a foreign land and 'every male slave is trained as a soldier'.[44] James knew that the Abyssinians were 'splendid fighters' who, having foiled British, French and most memorably Italian imperialism for almost forty years, were not now, he felt, going to 'tremble' before 'a single white man' like Mussolini, however powerful.[45]

There were other parallels that James undoubtedly noticed. San Domingo, with its 'mountain ranges'—on independence it took the name Haiti from 'Ayiti,' the Indian word for mountains—was similar in terrain to Abyssinia, which was 'a high plateau, strategically very powerful'.[46] The stage was surely set for what James hoped would be 'one of the most savage battles between Capitalism and its opponents', and he was determined to help the slaves liberate themselves from 'Imperialistic domination of any kind'. In *Black Jacobins* James described just why the slave revolt on San Domingo was so relevant. 'For self-sacrifice and heroism, the men, women and children who drove out the French stand second to no fighters for independence in any place or time. And the reason was simple. They had seen at last that without independence they could not maintain their liberty, and liberty was far more concrete for former slaves than the elusive forms of political democracy in France'.[47] Toussaint's achievement had been to help the slaves liberate themselves, and in the process transform themselves into an army capable of defeating the finest armies of that period.

James was prepared to use his study of Toussaint L'Ouverture's military strategy and tactics in the coming war. When the odds were against him in the fight against Napoleon's army, L'Ouverture had led a ruthless guerilla war. As James described in *Black Jacobins*, 'Toussaint, with half his 18,000 troops in the ranks of the enemy, could only delay and harass the advance, devastate the country and deprive Leclerc of supplies, while retiring slowly to the mountains...he would raid Leclerc's outposts, make surprise attacks, lay ambushes, give the French no peace, while avoiding major engagements. With the coming of the rains, the French, worn out, would fall victims in thousands to the fever, and the blacks would descend and drive them into the sea'.[48] Taking the example of the slaves on San Domingo as a guide to action, James argued that the Abyssinians should also employ a 'scorched earth' policy if necessary. As James argued at a public meeting of the IAFA on 16 August 1935, if the Abyssinians were defeated in the coming conflict, 'we look to them to destroy their country rather than hand it over to the invader. Let them burn down Addis Ababa, let them poison their wells and water holes, let them destroy every blade of vegetation.'[49] It is not surprising that by this time, after a few months of activity for the IAFA, James had turned his notes on the San Domingo revolt into a script for a play about its leader, *Toussaint L'Ouverture*.[50]

Marie Seton, a journalist and friend of James, brought the play to the attention of the Stage Society, 'a very exclusive society which had given first performances of Bernard Shaw and many other playwrights who became world famous'.[51] Their precondition for performing James's play was that Paul Robeson, the famous black African-American singer and actor, who was currently living in London, should play Toussaint. James had already met Robeson, who would often take his son to watch cricket matches at Lords, at various parties, and they had both been supporters of the League of Coloured Peoples.[52] However, Robeson's busy work commitments, and his growing commitment to the Communist International (which involved frequent trips to the Soviet Union) meant regular contact was impossible. Eventually, however James 'ran him down at some party, told him about it and he agreed to read the script. He read it and with great simplicity and directness said, yes, he would be ready to play the role: there were not too many parts in those days which gave a black actor, however distinguished, a role that lifted him above the servants' quarters'.[53] Robeson in fact had already had five offers to star in various plays about the Haitian revolution, and had even been planning to make a film, *Black Majesty*, with the Soviet film-maker Sergei Eisenstein. However, by 1935 Eisenstein was under censure by Stalin's regime and the project fell through. Perhaps that was an additional factor why Robeson, on the verge of going to the United States to film *Showboat*, promised to star in James's play on his return.[54]

War and the continuation of politics by other means

Whatever James's hopes for a repeat of the Haitian revolution in Abyssinia, the war proved to be completely different when it began in October 1935. The Haitian slave rebellion lasted twelve years and was, as James noted, 'one of the great epics of revolutionary struggle and achievement'.[55] Yet largely thanks to advanced military technology, particularly aircraft, Italy's colonial conquest of Abyssinia was effectively over in only six months. However much heroic resistance they mounted to the Italian invasion, without international aid and modern arms, the odds facing the Abyssinians were insurmountable. Signor Vittorio Mussolini, an Italian flying officer, has described the ruthlessness with which the Italians exploited their overwhelming military superiority. 'I dropped an aerial torpedo in the centre of the group [of Ethiopian horsemen] and the group spread out like a flowery rose...about fifty brigands had a taste of our splinters. It was most entertaining work and had a tragic but beautiful effect.'[56] While rebels did retreat to the mountains to conduct a guerrilla war, the Italians used poison gas bombs extensively to terrorise the rest of the population, even targeting the Red Cross, hospitals and other civilian targets.[57]

This is not the place to go through James's tremendous efforts to raise the question of the Abyssinians in Britain while the war was going on. As a member of the ILP, James wrote searing articles in their weekly paper, the *New Leader*, and went on an extensive speaking tour which took him for the first time to Wales, Scotland, Ireland.[58] He urged support for 'workers' sanctions', whereby industrial action would be taken to stop war materials going to Italy.

An article entitled 'Abyssinia and the Imperialists' that James wrote in early 1936 for *Keys*, journal of the League of Coloured People, gives a sense of what Abyssinia meant to him. 'Africans and people of African descent, especially those who have been poisoned by British imperialist education, needed a lesson. They have got it.' The article noted that 'the issue before us today is obscured by the mountain of lies and nonsense which are being wrapped around it', notably the notion of 'collective security' which the existence of the League of Nations conjured up. James cut through the idea that the world's two greatest imperialist powers, Britain and France, were motivated by the ideals of the League of Nations and their expressed desire to uphold 'the independence of Abyssinia'. In fact, he argued, 'these European imperialists have been after Abyssinia for years' and now 'every succeeding day shows exactly the real motives which move imperialism in its contact with Africa, shows the incredible savagery and duplicity of European imperialism in its quest for markets and raw materials'. Their duplicity was seen in the weak sanctions the League of Nations had belatedly imposed on Italy, and in the Hoare-Laval Pact of December 1935, which saw the British and

French Governments once again bypass the League to offer Mussolini most of Abyssinia under a 'peace' deal. James stressed that 'the only thing to save Abyssinia is the efforts of the Abyssinians themselves', together with international solidarity. James called for 'action by the great masses of Negroes and sympathetic whites and Indians all over the world, by demonstrations, public meetings, resolutions, financial assistance to Abyssinia, strikes against the export of all material to Italy, refusal to unload Italian ships, etc.'[59]

Following the negotiations between Italy, Britain and France over the colonial division of Abyssinia could only have strengthened James's understanding of the economic impulse behind the colonial rivalry of Britain, France and Spain for San Domingo. In February 1936 James took a break from intensive touring and speaking, and spent March making revolutionary propaganda against imperialism using the medium of radical theatre. Just how much the Abyssinian war had deepened James's understanding of the San Domingo revolution can be seen by an examination of his play, *Toussaint L'Ouverture*, which was shown in two performances on 15 and 16 March 1936 at the Westminster Theatre in London. As James noted in March 1936, when the French Revolution broke out in 1789, the French portion of San Domingo was 'the richest and most valuable colony in the world. Thirty thousand whites and a similar number of mulattoes controlled the production of vast wealth by the ruthless exploitation of half a million slaves.'[60] Its sugar industry, as he was to note in *Black Jacobins*, made it 'an integral part of the economic life of the age, the greatest colony in the world, the pride of France, and the envy of every other imperialist nation'.[61]

In *Toussaint L'Ouverture*, James highlighted how all the governments of the European colonial powers had the same interests in common. The words he put in the mouth of British general Maitland, when in private conversation with a representative of the French government, are typical:

I have spoken, not as an Englishman, not as an enemy of France, but as a white man and a representative of a colonial power with the same intentions as yours. As long as General Toussaint continues the way he is going, the prestige of the European in these colonies is in grave danger. And we rule as much by prestige as by arms. See what he calls himself now, 'Louverture', opener of a way for his people. At whose expense?[62]

The deserts of Abyssinia were a far less glittering prize, but imperial pride and power were still at stake for Italy, France and Britain.

James also satirised the duplicity of imperial diplomats. Perhaps thinking of how the British and French governments had promised to safeguard the

Abyssinians' independence while in private colluding with Mussolini, James now attacked the US government's 'non-intervention' in respect to San Domingo. When discussing the British government's wish to return to San Domingo and re-establish slavery when the time was right, the American consul Lear, stresses:

> my Government is not interested in colonial complications, gentlemen…it is trade my Government is interested in. If a substantial amount of trade can be provided to our men of business in New York then you can be sure my Government will look with sympathy upon any measures you may take to guarantee the dominance of the white race.

Lear agrees with Maitland's observation to him that, 'you know, Consul, in dealing with Orientals and men of colour, white men can never have the full confidence that we can have in another, for instance'. Yet by way of a joke, once it is clear that Toussaint is too strong for the re-imposition of slavery to be viable in the short term, Lear turns to Toussaint himself. 'My Government is not interested in the rivalry of colonial powers…all that we ask for is a fair share of the trade of San Domingo. If a substantial portion of that trade can be diverted from France to us, then you can be sure that my Government will look with sympathy upon any measures you may take to guarantee the independence of the blacks'.[63]

The ideology of 'humanitarianism', with a promise to liberate the slaves of Abyssinia, was used alongside open racism by Mussolini to justify his conquest. Fascist Italy's claims to be on a 'civilising mission' were given serious considered attention in Britain, and Lord Hardinge of Penhurst described the Abyssinians as 'a savage and barbarous enemy'. Lord Stanhope, Under-Secretary of State for Foreign Affairs, told a Foreign Office official that it would be wrong to sell the Abyssinians arms as that 'would be going back on the White Man everywhere'. On 15 July 1935 the *Daily Mail* asserted that 'in this war which now seems inevitable' the British people's 'sympathy is wholly with the cause of the white races, which Italy is so finely upholding'. The *Mail*'s foreign editor Ward Price went further, declaring Mussolini a 'genius' and warning that if we opposed Italy's expansion 'to one of the last and most backward of independent nation states, we should be hindering the progress of civilisation'.[64] The consequences of an Abyssinian victory were too alarming to consider. The Earl of Mansfield feared that 'should Italy lose, it would be at once a great encouragement to all that stands for mischief and sedition among the coloured races of the world'.[65] Racism was not new and, as James noted, had first developed in order to 'justify the abominable cruelties' the ruling colonists of the eighteenth century slave plantations practised. In *Black Jacobins*, James quoted a memoir of one colonial governor published in 1789 which noted 'the Negroes are unjust, cruel, barbarous, half-human, treacherous, deceitful, thieves, drunkards, proud, lazy, unclean, shameless, jealous to fury, and cowards'.[66] In his play, James attributed racist statements to representatives of the British, French and American governments as a matter of course.

Yet the play was also an attempt to highlight how the Haitian revolution had been victorious, and to drive the lessons he had learnt from the Abyssinian experience home. Many people had put their faith in the League of Nations, yet the 'collective security' of Britain, France and Russia had done nothing to safeguard Abyssinia. As Weisbord has noted, 'regrettably, the black world had the will but not the power to stem the tide of fascist aggression. Perhaps the greater tragedy is that the white world which had the power lacked the will.'[67] Leaving the major imperialist powers aside, the betrayal of Abyssinia by Stalinist Russia, since 1934, a member of the League of Nations, was particularly striking. As war loomed in 1935, Trotsky observed that it was 'an irony of history' that 'in the international arena, the government of the Soviet Union has become a conservative power. It is for the status quo, against change. But it has not lifted a finger for the status quo in Ethiopia.'[68] In fact, come war the Soviet Union did lift a finger, but only to tell the Abyssinians where they could go. The economic interests of the Russian oil industry came before any notion of calling for international working-class action. As Trotsky later remarked, while Litvinov 'expressed his gratitude to the diplomats of France and England for their efforts "in behalf of peace", efforts which so auspiciously resulted in the annihilation of Abyssinia, oil from the Caucausus continued to nourish the Italian fleet'.[69]

The defeat of Abyssinia, thanks in no small part to this betrayal, now brought home graphically to James the significance and importance of the great French revolution in general, and the Jacobins in particular, to the ultimate victory of the San Domingo slaves. The slave revolt on Haiti had been inextricably intertwined with another revolution, in France. Mild reforms to the slave system yielded in the first years of the French revolution by the assembly in Paris created the necessary space for the revolt on San Domingo in 1791. The slave rebellion in turn encouraged radicals in France to smash the power of the slave owning 'aristocrats of the skin' altogether. From then on, as James put it in *Black Jacobins*, 'to all the blacks, revolutionary France, which had decreed equality and the abolition of slavery, was a beacon…France was to them indeed the mother country'.[70] Many black anti-imperialist activists had, like Padmore and Kenyatta, taken 'Mother Russia' to their hearts in such a fashion, but when the news that Soviet Russia had sold oil to fascist Italy broke, many broke with Stalinism overnight. George Padmore, who had resigned his posts at the Comintern in 1934, described what happened to the communist-controlled League Against Imperialism, which was effectively killed as an organisation. 'The few Africans in London who were associated with the League through affiliated membership of the Negro Improvement Association, headed by Arnold Ward, a West Indian, severed their association with the Communists and helped to form the International African Friends of Abyssinia.'[71]

There could be no better audience for James's play *Toussaint L'Ouverture* than those black revolutionary activists who had just had their faith in Stalin's Russia shattered. Many of them were so disgusted at the betrayal that they began to retreat from revolutionary politics altogether, and fell into simply lobbying and placing demands on the British government.[72] James used his play about *Toussaint L'Ouverture* to counteract this tendency. As he wrote of Toussaint in *Black Jacobins*, 'in nothing does his genius stand out so much as refusing to trust the liberation of the blacks to the promises of French and British Imperialism'.[73] Indeed, 'it is easier to find decency, gratitude, justice, and humanity in a cage of starving tigers than in the councils of imperialism, whether in the cabinets of Pitt or Bonaparte, of Baldwin, Laval or Blum'.[74] In the play, Dessalines warns Toussaint of the imperialists' hidden agendas. 'Toussaint, you are too soft with these people. You will pay for it one day. Land for plantations—and slaves to work. That is their word, that is their God, that is their education, that is their religion…Don't trust the French. Don't trust the English. Don't trust the Americans. Trust the people. For freedom they will fight to the end.'[75]

That line was delivered to Paul Robeson, playing Toussaint L'Ouverture. Robert Hill contends that *Black Jacobins* would have been 'significantly different in quality in the absence of James's relationship to Robeson'. This was because 'at a very profound and fundamental level, Robeson as a man *shattered* James's colonial conception of the Black Physique…the magnificent stature of Robeson gave to him a new appreciation of the powerful and extraordinary capabilities which the African possessed, in both head and body'.[76] However, just as important, perhaps, was the way in which Robeson helped James understand Toussaint L'Ouverture's devout loyalty to the leaders of the French revolution. James now wondered at Robeson's 'complete commitment to the idea that something that was organised in Moscow and that came from Moscow was the only thing that could change the lives of black people in the United States'.[77] Part of the point of writing the play for James was to stress that Toussaint's fate was so closely tied to the French revolution that he did not have the political independence to avoid going down with it. As he put it in *Black Jacobins*, Toussaint's 'allegiance to the French revolution and all it opened up for mankind in general and the people of San Domingo in particular…had made him what he was. But in the end this ruined him.'[78]

The play itself put the black slaves' struggle centre stage in the liberation of Haiti. The *New Statesman* noted that James 'brings out effectively, though without exaggeration, the nobility of Toussaint's character and the treachery of the white men'.[79] However, Paul Robeson was the real star, both off and on the stage. Though the play was produced by Peter Godfrey, James remembers 'at times Godfrey was occupied and as the author I had to rehearse the cast. It was during those days that I had a good look at Paul and got to know him well.' Robeson, James felt, had 'that extraordinary combination of immense power enclosed in a pervading gentleness' and, despite his acting experience, was 'always ready to listen and to oblige'. The weeks in rehearsal with Robeson, whom James later regarded as 'the most remarkable human being I have ever met,' must have been one of the happiest times of James's life up to that point.[80] James remembers Robeson's 'physique and the voice, the spirit behind him' ensured that 'the moment he came onto the stage, the whole damn thing changed'. James even revised the play to let Robeson sing.[81] The *New Leader* noted that *Toussaint L'Ouverture* 'succeeds in convincing the audience that an Empire is nothing of which any white civilisation can be proud'.[82] Unfortunately, it was not shown in Italy where Mussolini was succeeding in convincing his people of the advantages of imperialism. Nor was it a topic Hollywood was keen to finance, despite Robeson's best efforts to turn the play into a film.[83]

Italy's war on Abyssinia made a deep impact on James's political development and on how he came to conceptualise the San Domingo revolution. One consequence of the Abyssinian war was to make another European war more likely than ever, as a more confident fascist Italy drew closer to a rearming and aggressive Nazi Germany. Yet James knew that the First World War had led to revolution, and he remained optimistic that another war would end in socialist revolution in Europe and colonial revolution internationally. His work with the IAFA, and the Pan-African movement more broadly, meant that by the time he settled down to write *Black Jacobins*, he 'had reached the conclusion that the centre of the Black revolution was Africa, not the Caribbean'.[84] As James's Toussaint L'Ouverture argued in the play, 'what the future holds for us I don't know. These whites are stronger than us, but they fight so much with one another that we can have hope for the future…we shall establish a base in Africa and from there fight the slave trade, that curse and degradation of our people'.[85] *Black Jacobins* was just as defiant. 'The imperialists envisage an eternity of African exploitation: the African is backward, ignorant…They dream dreams.'[86] After the defeat of Abyssinia, James's invocation of the spectre of the great Haitian revolution, according to Paul Foot 'perhaps the most glorious victory of the oppressed over their oppressors in all history', was needed more than ever.[87] It was a timely reminder that while Mussolini's troops may have won that battle, in the war for their liberation from colonialism, it was the workers and peasants of Africa who, in Aime Cesaire's words, really stood 'at the rendezvous of victory'. One wonders if the same could be said for those countries, and for Haiti itself, under American military and economic domination today.

Notes

1. J.R. Johnson, 'Why Negroes should oppose the war' in C.L.R. James et al., *Fighting Racism in World War II* (New York, 1990), pp.29–30. Johnson was one of James's pseudonyms, and the article appeared in *Socialist Appeal* in ten parts during September to October 1939.
2. C.L.R. James, *The Black Jacobins: Toussaint L'Ouverture and the San Domingo Revolution* (London, 2001), p.xviii.
3. Stuart Hall, 'Breaking Bread with History: C.L.R. James and The Black Jacobins', *History Workshop Journal*, 46 (1998), p.21.
4. C.L.R. James, 'The West Indian Intellectual', in J. J. Thomas, *Froudacity: West Indian fables explained* (London, 1969), p.26.
5. C.L.R. James, *Beyond a Boundary* (London, 1990), p.117. The offending article was by Sidney Harland and entitled 'Race Admixture' and it appeared in *The Beacon* in July 1931.
6. Anthony Bogues, *Caliban's Freedom: The early political thought of C.L.R. James* (London, 1997), p.21.
7. M.A.R.H.O. (ed.), *Visions of History* (Manchester, 1984), p.267; James, *Black Jacobins*, p.xv.
8. M.A.R.H.O. (ed.), *Visions of History*, p.267; Stuart Hall, 'A Conversation with C.L.R. James', in G. Farred (ed.), *Rethinking C.L.R. James* (Oxford, 1996), p.21.
9. James, *Black Jacobins*, p.xv.
10. C.L.R James, 'Slavery Today: A Shocking Exposure', *Tit-Bits*, 5 August 1933.
11. Kent Worcester has noted that James embraced Fabian political values as part of his intellectual evolution. See Kent Worcester, '"A Victorian with the rebel seed": C.L.R. James and the politics of intellectual engagement' in Alastair Hennesy (ed.), *Intellectuals in the Twentieth-Century Caribbean, vol. 1, Spectre of the new class* (London, 1992), p.115.
12. James, 'Slavery Today', *Tit-Bits*, 5 August 1933.
13. David Widgery, 'C.L.R. James' in D. Widgery, *Preserving Disorder: Selected essays 1968–88* (London, 1989), p.123. As James told Widgery in 1980, 'I realised the Stalinists were the greatest liars and corrupters of history there ever were. No

one convinced me of this. I convinced myself'.

14. James R. Hooker, *Black Revolutionary; George Padmore's path from Communism to Pan-Africanism* (London, 1967), p.23. See also Peter Fryer, *Staying Power: The history of black people in Britain* (London, 1987), p.334.

15. M.A.R.H.O. (ed.), *Visions of History*, p.269.

16. C.L.R. James, *At the Rendezvous of Victory: Selected writings*, vol.3 (London, 1984), p.207.

17. James, *Black Jacobins*, p.xv.

18. James, *At the Rendezvous of Victory*, p.207.

19. C.L.R. James, 'Interview with Al Richardson' (1986), *Revolutionary History*, www.revolutionary-history.co.uk/supplem/jamesint.htm. For James's description of workers' power in France in February 1934, see C.L.R. James, *World Revolution 1917–1936: The rise and fall of the Communist International* (London, 1937), p.379–81.

20. Robert G. Weisbord, *Ebony Kinship: Africa, Africans and the Afro-American* (London, 1973), p.89.

21. Articles X and XVI of the League of Nations Covenant laid down the principle that all League members should protect other members from external aggression and authorized moral, economic and military sanctions. See D. Waley, *British Public Opinion and the Abyssinian War 1935–6* (London, 1975), p.18. See also Paul Corthorn, 'The Labour Party and the League of Nations: The Socialist League's role in the sanctions crisis of 1935', *Twentieth Century British History*, 13, 1 (2002), pp.67, 70.

22. James, *At the Rendezvous of Victory*, p.230. See also Paget Henry and Paul Buhle (eds), *C.L.R. James's Caribbean* (London, 1992), p.8.

23. Barbara Bush, *Imperialism, Race and Resistance: Africa and Britain 1919–1945* (London, 1999), p.211.

24. James, *Beyond a Boundary*, p.250.

25. Bush, *Imperialism, Race and Resistance*, p.240.

26. Fryer, *Staying Power*, pp.340, 345. Amy Ashwood Garvey was honorary treasurer. For more on other leading members see George Padmore, *Pan-Africanism or Communism: The coming struggle for Africa* (London, 1956), p.145. The IAFA disbanded after 'major combat operations' had finished in Abyssinia and after others had formed the Abyssinian Association, active in April 1936. See Waley, *British Public Opinion and the Abyssinian war*, p.115.

27. *Manchester Guardian*, 29 July 1935.

28. *Manchester Guardian*, 30 July 1935.

29. C.L.R James, 'Black Intellectuals in Britain', in B. Parekh (ed.), *Colour, Culture and Consciousness* (London, 1974), p.158. James's memory serves him correctly here. See *The Times*, 29 July 1935 and S. Asante, *Pan-African Protest: West Africa and the Italo-Ethiopian crisis, 1934–1941* (London, 1977), p.46.

30. C.L.R James, *The Future in the Present: Selected writings*, vol.1 (London, 1977), p.114.

31. Waley, *British Public Opinion and the Abyssinian War*, p.20.

32. James, 'Black intellectuals in Britain', p.158.

33. James, 'Black intellectuals in Britain', p.158.

34. Cedric J. Robinson, *Black Marxism: The making of the black radical tradition* (New Jersey, 1991), p.381.

35. Konni Zilliacus, *Abyssinia* (London, 1935), p.6.

36. James, 'Black intellectuals in Britain', p.159.

37. Asante, *Pan-African Protest*, p.46. In a letter to the *New Leader*, 3 June 1936, James described how he offered through the Abyssinian embassy 'to take service under the Emperor, military or otherwise'. The ambassador, Dr Martin, advised him 'that he thought my work with the International Friends of Ethiopia would better serve the struggle against Italy'. This letter is reprinted in James, 'Black intellectuals in Britain', pp.158–9.

38. Farred (ed.), *Rethinking C.L.R. James*, p.109.

39. *New Leader*, 3 June 1936.

40. James, *Black Jacobins*, p.295.

41. *New Leader*, 3 June 1936.

42. C.L.R. James, *Nkrumah and the Ghana Revolution* (London, 1977), p.66.

43. James, *Black Jacobins*, p.xviii.

44. Waley, *British Public Opinion and the Abyssinian War*, p.46; James, 'Slavery Today', *Tit-Bits*, 5 August 1933.

45. C.L.R. James, 'Abysinnia and the Imperialists' in Anna Grimshaw (ed.), *The C.L.R. James Reader* (Oxford, 1992), p.64.

46. James, *Black Jacobins*, p.22; Kent Worcester, *C.L.R. James: A political biography* (New York, 1996), p.34; Grimshaw (ed.), *C.L.R. James Reader*, p.64.

47. James, *Black Jacobins*, p.288.

48. James, *Black Jacobins*, p.248.

49. Asante, *Pan-African Protest*, p.46.

50. By October, he had written the script; see 'Play by an ILPer', *New Leader*, 25 October 1935.

51. C.L.R. James, 'Paul Robeson: Black Star' in C.L.R. James, *Spheres of Existence: Selected writings*, vol. 2 (London, 1980), p.257. Act II, Scene I of the original play was published in *Life and Letters Today* in Spring 1936. James is described in this as 'a Negro writer, born in the West Indies in 1901. After teaching and miscellaneous journalism, he came to England in 1932. He writes for the *Manchester Guardian* and other papers. He hopes to publish next year a political study of Toussaint L'Ouverture and the Haitian Revolution'. See *Life and Letters Today*, 14, 3 (1936), p.211. For a cast list, see J.P. Wearing, *The London Stage, 1930–1939*, vol.2 (London, 1990).

52. Bush, *Imperialism, Race and Resistance*, p.214.

53. James, 'Paul Robeson: Black Star', p.257.

54. Marie Seton, *Sergei M. Eisenstein* (London, 1952), p.352. Martin B. Duberman, *Paul Robeson* (London, 1989) pp.194, 633. Eisenstein had wanted to make a film about the Haitian revolution since 1931, but he could not get financial backing from Hollywood, where he was at the time. As he told his Russian film students in 1935, 'when I was in America I wanted to make a film of this rising in Haiti, but it was impossible; nowadays Haiti is virtually a colony of the USA.' See

Ronald Bergan, *Eisenstein* (London, 1997), p.267. Haiti was under US military occupation from 1915 to 1934. Plus ça change.

55. James, *Black Jacobins*, p.xviii.

56. Viscount Cecil, *A Great Experiment* (London, 1941), p.267.

57. Alberto Sbacelli, *Legacy of Bitterness: Ethiopia and Fascist Italy 1935–41* (Eritrea, 1997), p.55.

58. John Archer, 'C.L.R. James in Britain, 1932–38', *Revolutionary History*, 6, 2/3 (1996), p.61.

59. Grimshaw (ed.), *C.L.R. James Reader*, pp.63–4, 66. The article was originally published in *Keys*, 3, 5 (January-March 1936).

60. C.L.R. James, 'Toussaint L'Ouverture' in *Life and Letters Today*, 14, 3 (1936), p.7. This is a publication of Act II, Scene I of *Toussaint L'Ouverture*, with an introduction by James. A copy of the manuscript of the original production is among the papers of British Trotskyist Jock Haston at the University of Hull [DJH/21]. For a revised version of the play performed in the 1960s see 'Toussaint L'Ouverture [Black Jacobins]' in Grimshaw (ed.), *C.L.R. James Reader*.

61. James, *Black Jacobins*, p.xviii.

62. James, 'Toussaint L'Ouverture', p.7.

63. James, 'Toussaint L'Ouverture', pp.9, 13, 15.

64. Waley, *British Public Opinion and the Abyssinian War*, p.23.

65. Waley, *British Public Opinion and the Abyssinian War*, p.76.

66. James, *Black Jacobins*, p.13.

67. Weisbord, *Ebony Kinship*, p.110.

68. Leon Trotsky, *Writings, 1935–6* (New York, 1970), p.5.

69. Leon Trotsky, *The Revolution Betrayed* (New York, 1989), p.195. In *World Revolution*, p.387–9, James outlined the steady retreat of the foreign policy of the Soviet Union with respect to Abyssinia, and how initial support for 'workers' sanctions' became replaced by support for the action by the League of Nations alone.

70. James, *Black Jacobins*, p.174.

71. Padmore, *Pan-Africanism or Communism*, p.330.

72. James criticised George Padmore's *How Britain Rules Africa* (1936) on these grounds. James wrote that parts of it were 'grievously disappointing' as Padmore talks about Britain 'as if he were some missionary or Labour politician'. Instead, James insisted 'Africans must win their own freedom. Nobody will win it for them'. See *New Leader*, 29 May 1936 and Robinson, *Black Marxism*, p.383.

73. James, *Black Jacobins*, p.195.

74. James, *Black Jacobins*, p.229.

75. James, 'Toussaint L'Ouverture', pp.16–17.

76. Hill, 'In England, 1932–1938', in Buhle (ed.), *C.L.R. James*, pp.73–4.

77. James, *At the Rendezvous of Victory*, p.196.

78. James, *Black Jacobins*, p.236. Toussaint was captured and killed by the French in 1803 when they betrayed his trust.

79. *New Statesman*, 21 March 1936.

80. James, 'Paul Robeson', pp.257–8. See also James, *At the Rendezvous of Victory*,

p.207. James took a small walk-on part in *Toussaint L'Ouverture*; see Fryer, *Staying Power*, p.337.

81. Duberman, *Paul Robeson*, p.197; James, 'Paul Robeson', pp.257–8.

82. *New Statesman*, 21 March 1936; *New Leader*, 20 March 1936. For other reviews, see *Era*, 18 March 1936; *Observer*, 22 March 1936; *Stage*, 19 March 1936; *Evening Standard*, 17 March 1936; *Daily Herald*, 17 March 1936; *Sunday Times*, 22 March 1936; *The Times,* 17 March 1936. As James noted, 'when the play was performed, he [Robeson], if not it, was a great success'. See James, 'Paul Robeson', p.258. The *New Statesman* drama critic, while praising Robeson's 'thoughtful perfor-mance', described the production as 'rough rather than ready, but we doubt if the play, respectable though it is, could ever be very impressive'. When this rather hostile reviewer criticised James's portrayal of Christophe, James referred him to the historical record in the next issue. See *New Statesman*, 28 March 1936. The play also 'made history' in another sense. As Michael McMillan has noted, 'since the 19th century, black perfomers have graced the English stage' but 'if we are to talk of black theatre as a movement, as a body of work written by, produced, directed, and performed by black people, C.L.R. James's play, *The Black Jacobins*, produced in the 1930s, signifies that beginning'. See A.R. Thompsett (ed.), *Black Theatre in Britain* (Amsterdam, 1996), p.58.

83. As James remembers, 'Paul was pleased. We agreed that we should seek ways and means to do it commercially. "I can play Toussaint and you will play Dessalines, and later we can switch"…but at that time Paul was headed towards Moscow and I, as a Trotskyist, was most definitely anti-Moscow. We knew about each other and never quarreled, but the idea of doing the play automatically faded into nothing'. See James, 'Paul Robeson', p.259. For Robeson's battle with Hollywood, see Duberman, *Paul Robeson*, pp.196–7; Schwarz, 'Black Metropolis, White England' in Nava, and O'Shea (eds), *Modern Times*, p.186.

84. M.A.R.H.O. (ed.), *Visions of History*, p.267. In March 1936, James was aiming 'to publish next year a political study of Toussaint Louverture' and had secured an advance from the publisher Methuen. See James, 'Toussaint L'Ouverture', p.211 and C.L.R. James, 'Lectures on The Black Jacobins', in *Small Axe*, 8 (2000), p.70. However, *Black Jacobins* was not published in 1937, but in 1938, and by Secker and Warburg rather than Methuen. In mid-1936, via his contacts in the ILP, James had met Frederic Warburg, of the publishers Secker and Warburg, who asked him if he would consider writing a book on 'African Socialism'. James told him 'No, that is not the book for me'. Instead James wanted to write about 'the mess that is taking place in Russia and the explosions that are going to take place soon—this was before the first Moscow Trials [August 1936]'. That work became *World Revolution*. Secker and Warburg published *Minty Alley* in late 1936, a novel James had written in Trinidad in 1929.

85. James, 'Toussaint L'Ouverture', p.17.

86. James, *Black Jacobins*, p.303.

87. Paul Foot, 'The Black Jacobins', *New Statesman*, 2 February 1979.

The Abyssinia Crisis, British Labour and the Fracturing of the Anti-War Movement

Andrew Flinn and Gidon Cohen

Much of the orthodox labour and communist historiography of the 1930s emphasises the continuity of the left's anti-fascist credentials, in explicit contrast to those on the right, notably ministers in the National Government and other members of the Conservative elite. In this account the left was not tainted by association with appeasement. The Abyssinian crisis assumes central significance in this context because it marked the point when the labour movement first fully expressed its principled anti-fascism, a stance maintained through the Spanish Civil War and culminating in the anti-fascist struggle of 1939–45.[1] A major theme of this writing has been to stress the ideological isolation of the most resolutely anti-war sections of the British left after 1935, often conflating pacifism with the distinct arguments of anti-war socialism.[2] An alternative historiography to be found within the international relations literature presents a different picture, stressing the left's powerful attachment to pacifism and hence appeasement. This was perhaps most notably symbolised by the former Labour leader George Lansbury's meetings with Hitler, but also by the divisions in the movement over whether to support the National Government on the defence estimates, rearmament and peacetime conscription.[3]

Taking these two views of the labour movement's attitude to war as our context, this article seeks to provide a more nuanced understanding of the impact of the Abyssinian crisis on the British movement. The debates over the significance of Abyssinia have been constructed almost entirely through a discussion of prominent individuals, most notably in the opposition of Ernest Bevin and George Lansbury. The analysis presented here provides an alternative view of responses to the crisis by looking at both leadership and rank-and-file responses to the crisis within the Independent Labour Party (ILP) and the Socialist League. The article also highlights the way in which the particulars of these discussions were important in influencing the institutional responses to the crisis, which in turn were crucial in shaping responses to later events. By looking briefly at other developments in the anti-war and pacifist movements in the late 1930s, focusing in particular on the Women's Co-operative Guild, we point to the ways in which the intra- and inter-institutional alliances that were formed in the context of the First World War and broken in 1935 shaped the possibilities for the British left in the later 1930s.

Central to our argument is the importance of distinguishing between dif- ferent, yet equally deeply rooted, anti-war views in the British labour movement. These positions encompassed pacifist traditions but were also, particularly on the left, much broader in scope and not limited to pacifism. It is important to recognise and to differentiate between these beliefs. The most acute studies on the attitudes of inter-war labour movement activists to war and peace are not by labour historians but by a historian of the peace and the anti-war movements, Martin Ceadel. Over the course of several books, Ceadel has identified a number of separate trends in the labour move- ment. First were those, often from a Christian socialist background, who advocated an absolute pacifism. Second were those whom Ceadel refers to as 'pacificists' who sought to oppose war as far as possible but did not renounce recourse to violence as a last resort. Third were those referred to as 'defencists', who believed that the best means to minimise or prevent inter- national conflict was through strong defence and collective security.[4]

In the 1930s the 'defencists' who called for rearmament and a more aggressive response to the threats from fascism triumphed within the labour movement. This article will concern itself with those within the movement who, in opposition to the defencist line, continued to advocate an anti-war strategy. This anti-war section was not merely pacifist but included an influ- ential strain that, while opposing imperialist and capitalist wars, supported ideas of class or revolutionary warfare and whose adherents were to be found in and around the Labour Party of the 1930s, in organisations like the dis- affiliated ILP, the Socialist League and the Independent Socialist Party (ISP). For a long period the Communist Party of Great Britain (CPGB) had been among the leading advocates of war resistance, sponsoring organisations such as the British Anti-War Movement. But after 1934, following shifts in the USSR's foreign policy, most notably in its attitude to the League of Nations, British communists took up positions that, in this case at least, were similar to those of the defencists within the Labour leadership.

The 1935 Labour conference marked not only the triumph of the advo- cates of collective security over the pacifists within the party, but also over a left-wing anti-imperialist, anti-capitalist war opposition located inside and outside the party's ranks. One way to view the foreign or peace policy of the labour movement in the 1930s is that under the pressures of the growing fascist threat the inherently unstable alliance between the absolute pacifists, left-wing anti-war supporters and advocates of the League of Nations and collective security—an alliance that had held together since the 1920s—fell apart. For many on the left the contradictions of being both against war and against fascism became too great to sustain and as a result the anti-war movement was weakened and deeply divided. One example of this is the extent to which the otherwise impeccably moderate and orthodox Labour leadership of the Women's Co-operative Guild found itself isolated from its natural political allies by its rigid pacifist position. Furthermore it was unable to fall back on its traditional allies on the Labour left, in the ILP and the No More War Movement, because the terms of the compromises between the advocates of revolutionary and class war, on the one hand, and the pacifists over Abyssinia, on the other, rendered alliances much less likely in the rapidly changing international environment of the late 1930s. By the time that Britain declared war in September 1939, anti-war activists in the labour movement found themselves in a fractured and marginalised minority. This was comprised of ideological pacifists (often religious in inspiration), small socialist groupings whose opposition to the war was based on the rejection of imperialist war rather than of war *per se* and, from October, the British Communist Party, whose twists and turns on this matter had made them for many an uncongenial and untrustworthy ally. Any alliance between these groups was inherently unstable and riven by division. An analysis of the debates about how the working-class movement should respond to Italian fascist aggression in Abyssinia enables us to develop our understanding of the nature and extent of these divisions.

The Labour Party and Abyssinia

Immediately after the First World War, the labour movement appeared to unify around a peace policy that incorporated elements of support for disarmament, collective security through the League of Nations and, at times, war resistance. For the most part this compromise satisfied both absolute pacifists and the pacificists.[5] Although the left was deeply critical of the imperialist nature of the League, until it was tested the movement's unity held on this issue. It was not until the 1930s, when the failure of the World Disarmament Conference and the challenges by Japan, Germany and Italy to the post-war settlement meant that the implications of what collective security and the League of Nations actually entailed could no longer be ignored. It became increasingly difficult to deny that armed force was essential for collective security to restrain or defeat acts of international aggression. Some in the peace movement argued for the creation of an international army or police force under League control, but in reality this meant sanctioning the use of force by the National Government. Mainstream Labour opinion, including the growing numbers of defencists, supported the notion of collective security allied to significantly rearmed defences. However for a number of pacifists and for the anti-war left, including prominent figures such as Lansbury and Cripps, this was an unwelcome development. Before matters came to a head, party policy could be contradictory. The 1933 Labour conference was concerned primarily with disputes over domestic issues. Faced with these preoccupations, the leadership had accepted unopposed a Socialist League motion committing the party to a general strike and mass resistance to any war called by the National Government. At the same it reiterated its support for the League of Nations and multilateral disarmament. Charles Trevelyan, former President of the Board of Education and founder member of the Union of Democratic Control, moved the resolution and also wrote a Socialist League pamphlet, *Mass Resistance to War*. Although the proposal for a general strike did not find much favour amongst the trade unions, it was not considered to be immediately relevant and so was not directly challenged until the following year. At that time the Trades Union Congress (TUC) General Council stated that in certain circumstances it would be willing to support the government in 'defensive action taken to preserve the nation, and its democratic institutions'. The new policy was confirmed at the 1934 Labour Conference where the left's position was defeated on a wide range of issues. A clear commitment to the League of Nations and collective security was written into the 'War and Peace' section of the party's new policy programme, *For Socialism and Peace*.[6]

In 1932 the ILP, the largest of the Labour Party's socialist societies, had disaffiliated from the Labour Party after failing to achieve a satisfactory accommodation over the pursuit of socialist objectives and constitutional freedoms within the parliamentary Labour Party. After the ILP's disaffiliation, the main grouping of left socialists within the party was the Socialist League. Formed in 1932, and including many former ILP members who had decided not to leave Labour, the Socialist League's policy regarding war and the League of Nations remained unequivocal. They pledged to 'neither fight nor in any way help in such a war, nor to support any policies or actions that put the interests of a mis-called patriotism before those of the workers throughout the world'. In event of war, they maintained, a general strike should be used in order to press for a revolutionary change in society. They were committed to making the League of Nations 'an effective instrument for the promotion of international peace, co-operation and total disarmament'. But this did not include support for use of the League for the pursuance of the imperialist agenda of capitalist governments like the National Government. Rather international peace was to be sought through close alliance with the USSR, pacts of non-aggression and disarmament. The most recent historian of the Socialist League has argued that its attitudes to war and foreign policy were heavily influenced by the formulations of J. A. Hobson and H. N. Brailsford on the role of imperialism and capitalism as the causes of war and that these precluded support for actions of imperialist governments through organisations like the League of Nations. Despite the similarities of their policies and their criticisms of the national Labour policy, the Socialist League denied any co-operation or joint action with the ILP.[7]

The growing divisions between the advocates of collective security, pacifism and opposition to war were thrown into sharper relief as the situation in Abyssinia became increasingly serious through the summer and autumn of 1935. 'Defencists' such as Ernest Bevin, general secretary of the Transport and General Workers' Union, and Hugh Dalton, member of Labour's National Executive Committee (NEC), were emboldened by their success at the 1934 conference in defeating the left and by the results of the League of Nations Union Peace Ballot, which showed wide public support for collective security and use of sanctions to deter aggressor nations. Facing an imminent general election in a context of impending Italian aggression, the Labour leadership was determined to commit the party and the movement to a mainstream, patriotic position on the country's defence and international interests.

Inside the Labour Party, the debates about support for League sanctions and their possible consequences initially had little resonance beyond the Socialist League. The League's leader and a prominent left-wing figure in the Labour Party, Sir Stafford Cripps, called for preparations 'for mass resistance to war by workers of this country' at the League's June 1935 conference but at the AGM of the National Union of Railwaymen (NUR) a few weeks later there were few dissenting voices to the leadership line. Although union president Joseph Henderson ritualistically protested 'against alliances and treaties being made in our name', the conference backed the general secretary and Labour loyalist John Marchbank in defending official Labour movement policy relating to collective security and the League of Nations. In common with other trade union leaders, Marchbank was extremely cynical about the advocacy by the political left of a general strike, which left the 'responsibility for stopping war…upon the Trade Union Movement alone.'[8]

The implications of the crisis and the commitments made by the party leadership became clearer at the September TUC in Margate and the divisions began to widen. Conference debated a statement on the international crisis that had been agreed at a joint meeting of the three executives of the Labour Party, the Parliamentary Party and the TUC General Council immediately preceding the congress. The resolution declared 'its resolute faith in a collective peace system', while still reserving the right to take emergency measures should they be required. The declaration on the crisis committed Congress to support 'any action consistent with the principles and statutes of the League to restrain the Italian Government'. TUC General Secretary Walter Citrine left the delegates no doubt that support for League sanctions 'may mean war…there is no real alternative now left to us but the applying of sanctions involving in all probability, war'.

Some individual dissenting voices were heard, among them delegates from the mining, the engineering and the distributive workers' unions. George Crane, an engineer and member of the CPGB, called for greater recognition of the National Government's lack of trustworthiness, but TUC leaders sought to embarrass the left by emphasising the support offered to their policy by the Soviet Union. Outside the CPGB, others on the left acknowledged the ironies of the present situation. G.M. Hann, a Shop Assistants' delegate, mocked the new 'united front' of the Labour Party, the National Government, the CPGB and the Christian church. There were flashes of real anger and passion in the debate. One delegate vowed that he would only let his boy 'fight for the proletariat' and argued that the movement should seek to persuade the workers that 'This is not your war.' In his *Labour Monthly* article James Figgins, at that time a radical rank-and-file NUR leader, called for 'uncompromising opposition to sanctions' and derided the Labour leadership for offering working-class support for the imperialist foreign policy of the National Government. Perhaps drawing on his own past as a conscientious objector during the First World War, Figgins's arguments were more in tune with those advanced by the ILP, the Socialist League or by J.P.M. Millar in *The Plebs* and other left-wing critics of the League than with his usual allies in the CPGB. Nevertheless these sorts of arguments were very much in the minority; they were typically made by delegates speaking in a personal capacity, and not on behalf of their organisation. The General Council's resolution was overwhelmingly approved by 2,962,000 to 177,000.[9]

Thus, the congress confirmed the policy in support of the collective security agreed by the executives of the Labour Party, the Parliamentary Party and the TUC General Council. In response, the Socialist League announced that it would be holding meetings in September in several important towns and cities around the country to organise mass resistance to sanctions and war. Although it sought to demonstrate otherwise, it was clear that the league was now being forced to operate as a 'semi-independent' organised opposition within the Labour Party. While senior Labour figures were invited to speak at these meetings and put the party's case—J. R. Clynes spoke for the party in Manchester—many Labour affiliated organisations began to withdraw from the conferences rather than be seen as associating with anti-party events.

The message of the meetings appears to have been confused. In London, in a meeting much disrupted by local communists, Cripps himself spoke and advocated economic but not military League of Nations sanctions against Italy. Elsewhere some meetings voted for League policy while others rejected the Socialist League completely.[10] Crucial to these confusions were, according to Corthorn, the divisions within the Socialist League itself over the correct policy relating to the USSR and the difference made by Soviet entry into the League of Nations. Some of the Socialist League's leaders like William Mellor and Cripps considered Soviet participation in the League of Nations an irrelevancy or a tactical manoeuvre. Other prominent figures, notably J. T. Murphy, Trevelyan, and D. N. Pritt, opposed the official Socialist League line because of their support for the USSR. In this respect, they were closer to the CPGB, which following the USSR's entry in the autumn of 1934 had moderated its habitual hostility to the League and now advocated the use of League-imposed sanctions to prevent or restrain Italian aggression.[11] Others, like Aneurin Bevan and Brailsford were also ambivalent about the attitude taken to the League of Nations. A week before the Labour Party conference Brailsford wrote an article in *Reynold's News* that criticised the left's opposition to sanctions and argued for opposing British imperialism at the same time as opposing brutal regimes in Italy and elsewhere. Foot notes that Bevan did not speak in the debate on the crisis at Labour's conference and wonders whether this was due to his failure to catch the eye of the chair or perhaps more convincingly because 'he had doubts about the line to which the Left had committed itself.' These divisions were also likely to have been reflected amongst its ordinary membership.[12]

After the votes at the TUC and the Socialist League's conferences opposing sanctions and Labour movement policy, it was clear to contemporary commentators that further conflict was inevitable at Labour's Brighton conference. Both the party leader George Lansbury and his 'defencist' opponents appeared determined to resolve the issue of Lansbury's palpable unhappiness as a pacifist at being asked to endorse party policies with which he was in fundamental moral disagreement. The party's leader in the House of Lords, Lord Ponsonby, was in a similar dilemma. Ponsonby resigned shortly before the conference and Lansbury shortly after. Cripps also took a stand by resigning from the NEC so he could publicly oppose party policy without being a party spokesman, an act that simply confirmed his opponents' view of his unreliability and disloyalty.[13]

The opposition to sanctions came from two distinct but not necessarily mutually exclusive sources, pacifists such as George Lansbury, Lord Ponsonby and Lucy Cox and the anti-imperialists in the Socialist League. The former group stressed the personal dimension and the strength of their convictions. Lansbury told the conference that he had known since he was a small boy 'that force is no remedy'. Ponsonby, as a former Liberal who had opposed the 1914–18 war, reminded his audience of the length and consistency with which he had held his opinions, remarking that it was 'not a question of getting a gun out of a man's hand, it is a question of getting the idea out of his head which makes him want to use his gun.' Lansbury himself was welcomed with warm applause and listened to with respect causing Bevin to warn the conference not to be swayed by 'sentiment or personal attachment' and instructing the elderly party leader to stop taking his 'conscience round from body to body asking to be told what to be done with it'. A report in the *Manchester Guardian* stated that many delegates judged Bevin's speech to have been harsh but necessarily cruel. Despite the rejection of the anti-war position, within the party there remained widespread sympathy and tolerance for Lansbury and the other pacifists as individuals with sincerely held beliefs. This was demonstrated by those like Herbert Morrison and Charles Dukes, who while now firmly on the right of the party had both opposed the First World War, making public appeals for the tolerance of individual pacifists within the party.[14] The critical point was not that of tolerance for pacifists as individuals, but the problem posed by having a principled pacifist as Labour Party leader.

No such sympathy was extended to those like Cripps, William Mellor and other Socialist Leaguers who sought to oppose party policy on the crisis from the left. While the conference is generally remembered for the attack on Lansbury, Bevin and others directed as much of their fire at Cripps. In the debate Cripps denounced the League of Nations as 'the tool of satiated imperialist powers' and an 'International Burglars' Union'. He urged the Labour movement not to betray the British working class to imperialism but to work for the overthrow of the National Government and the implementation of workers' sanctions. Whatever the merits of his arguments, his case was undermined by the use made by Dalton, Marchbank and others of quotations from Cripps in support of the League and armed intervention to prevent aggressor nations. Cripps responded that he had revised his position because the changes in the League's membership had left it ever more firmly in the hands of the imperial powers. But the damage to his arguments in terms of consistency and trustworthiness was hard to repair. Trade-union leaders further resented the implication that in place of League sanctions, Cripps and his allies were suggesting working-class sanctions or mass action without any understanding of the consequences of such actions. Charles Dukes of the General and Municipal Workers castigated

> those people who have no idea as to what those people think—people who have no authority, no responsibility, no influence—talking in this conference as though it were possible to organise mass action against political action.

Referring back to the events of 1931, much of Bevin's real invective was directed not against Lansbury but against lawyers and middle-class intellectuals who could not be trusted and who like MacDonald had 'stab[bed] us in the back'. J. Williams of the Miners' Federation went further by likening Cripps to Sir Oswald Mosley. A consistent part of the trade-union criticism aimed at both the pacifists and the intellectuals of the Socialist League was that their lack of appreciation of the importance of collective responsibility and democratic representation in the Labour movement as opposed to personal morality or political ideology made them unreliable individualists whose ultimate loyalty to the movement was in question. Equally damaging to the anti-war left was the lack of support from other members of the Socialist League and the wider left. The Soviet Union's shift with regards to collective security and membership in the League of Nations persuaded even a former Union of Democratic Control member like Charles Trevelyan to support the League of Nations and oppose Cripps. Another leftist delegate, Dorothy Woodman, who also had strong pro-Soviet feelings, argued that by accusing the League of imperialism, Cripps, Mellor and others were by implication condemning the USSR of the same. When the matter was put to a vote, the opponents of party policy received only 102,000 votes as against 2,168,000 for the Executive. The trade union's 'necessary "plain speaking"' meant that the party had been 'purified and strengthened by unions' insistence upon loyalty and discipline in the leadership as well as among the rank and file.' Nevertheless the vote did not reflect the extent of the real divisions and unease over the direction the party was going.[15] At this critical moment two issues came together. One was the substantive question of the appropriate Labour Party response towards Italian aggression against Abyssinia. The second concerned the party's procedures and identity. This focussed on the proper relationship of the trade unions vis-à-vis politicians, a matter of great sensitivity since the defection of Ramsay MacDonald and his allies in 1931.

The scale of the defeats for those who advocated the anti-war line at both the TUC and Labour Conferences might suggest that support for pacifism or war resistance was insignificant within the Labour movement. But there were areas and arenas where the position held considerable influence. Under pressure of events, many who had originally supported anti-war positions were reluctantly starting to acknowledge the need to sanction collective security and armed resistance to fascism. But the trade union block votes in conference probably diminished the extent to which there was still residual support for pacifism and militant anti-war policies amongst local parties. To take one example, preparations for the general election in the Stockport Labour movement were severely disrupted by the fall-out from the local party's strong support for the Socialist League's anti-war line. The Stockport Socialist League branch shared personnel with the Independent Socialist Party, an organisation that had been formed as a result of disputes within the ILP.[16] The Socialist League branch along with an active core of militant NUR members took the lead in advocating a policy of war resistance and working-class sanctions.[17] Stockport was a dual member constituency, and its two prospective parliamentary candidates had diametrically different political attitudes on the subject of Abyssinia and the League of Nations. One candidate was Jenny Adamson, Labour Party chairwoman for 1935 and a senior member of the NEC and the Standing Joint Committee of Industrial Working Women's Organisations. The other was a Quaker pacifist and former ILP member, James Hudson. Even before he spoke at Labour Party conference against the NEC and Labour leadership, Hudson had publicly warned against 'Citrine's policy of out-Heroding Herod'. At a subsequent emergency meeting of the Stockport Trades Council and Labour Party, the party opposed sanctions as 'but a prelude to an imperialistic war' and pledged to 'organise mass resistance to war'. The meeting was not attended by Adamson but Hudson expressed complete support for Lansbury and his policies. Soon after the conference, and only weeks before the general election it was announced that due to the attitude of Mr Hudson and the local party, Mrs Adamson was resigning as parliamentary candidate for Stockport. Another candidate, Christopher Douthwaite, was adopted at the last minute but the party was soundly beaten by the National Government candidates.

Subsequently the local party once again pledged 'themselves in the interests of Party unity, to cease from indulging in personalities and peccadilloes'.[18] Events in Stockport may not have been typical of local Labour parties. But they suggest, particularly as the party sought to recover from the disastrous losses of 1931, that such splits and controversies were potentially extremely damaging.

Recognising the seriousness of the conference defeat and its own divisions, the Socialist League quickly issued a statement that it would remain in the party but that in the interests of unity, it would accept its defeat and no longer campaign against sanctions.[19] In any case, spurred on by this defeat and by events in Spain, within a year Cripps and other Socialist League leaders would be seeking an alliance with the communists and active intervention against fascism. On the other hand, many pacifists like Lansbury were unable to abandon their beliefs. Indeed after resigning from the Labour leadership, Lansbury concentrated his political endeavours in organisations like the Peace Pledge Union (PPU) attempting to prevent war. Commenting on events, and more sympathetic to the rebels than most unions, an editorial in the Amalgamated Engineering Union's (AEU) *Monthly Journal* recognised the seriousness of the divisions in the movement over the League of Nations and war, but emphasised that this was dissent based on principle. The two sides needed, it argued, to be reconciled without damage to the movement. Here in essence was the crux of the argument. If dissent from supporting the League and collective security was expressed as a matter of personal morality (that is, pacifism) it could be tolerated. But attempts that sought to change party policy in favour of either a pacifist or a socialist, anti-imperialist and anti-capitalist war position were to be firmly resisted.[20]

The Independent Labour Party and the Abyssinian crisis

Debates over Abyssinia within the Labour Party were consciously, if in some cases misleadingly, construed as a matter of personal morality. The politics of the ILP, which was still in the process of developing a new revolutionary policy following disaffiliation, made such an option less obviously available. Although in the longer term the same issues came to haunt the ILP, initially the party did not appear to show any need of a similar accommodation. Even as Italy was mobilising troops and threatening Abyssinian borders in early 1935, the ILP, in its journal the *New Leader*, was already attempting to make clear its position on the impending crisis, identifying the cause of the Abyssinian dispute as the rival imperialist interests of the different countries, with the focus firmly on their economic interests.[21]

As the crisis accelerated in September, the ILP, inspired by memories of its heroic opposition to the 1914–18 war, began mobilisation against another 'Capitalist and Imperialist war' that it uncompromisingly opposed, 'whether sanctioned by the League of Nations or not.' The newly created inner executive of the party, controlled by the parliamentary group, immediately issued an anti-war declaration signed by the MPs James Maxton, John McGovern and Campbell Stephen calling for 'maximum opposition' to the National Government's policy on the crisis.[22] The ILP's National Administrative Committee (NAC) released a further manifesto also calling for working-class mobilisation:

> Refuse to support the National Government in imposing sanctions or waging War for British Capitalism and Imperialism!
> Carry on the struggle against the National Government, Capitalism, Imperialism and War!
> Carry on the struggle for Workers' Power and Socialism![23]

Across the country the ILP launched itself enthusiastically into a 'Resist the War' campaign and thousands of working-class organisations were circularised with an anti-war letter signed by Maxton and ILP General Secretary Fenner Brockway.[24] Since disaffiliation in 1932 the ILP had been crippled by factional disputes. The attempts of the communist-inclined Revolutionary Policy Committee (RPC) to persuade the ILP to affiliate to the Communist International (Comintern) and join forces with the CPGB proved particularly divisive. By 1935 there was also a small but vocal Trotskyist presence within the ILP. However, the response to the crisis appeared to unite opposing factions. In London, the heart of factional activity, an emergency committee even managed to bring together Jack Gaster, Hilda Vernon and Carl Cullen of the RPC, Bert Matlow of the Trotskyist Marxist Group and John Aplin, a strident opponent of factions within the party.[25] To many activists the crisis appeared to re-invigorate the party. The ILP's initial response seemed to be principled and united. The crisis quickly became an important focal point for ILP propaganda and the *New Leader* gave prominence to a large number of articles on events including those written by the Marxist Group leader C.L.R. James calling for workers' sanctions.[26] Galvanised by a degree of support from outside the ILP, including a front-page article by key Scottish Labour Party figure Thomas Johnston in the Scottish Labour newspaper *Forward*, the workers' sanctions line increasingly identified primarily with the ILP assisted with party mobilisation.[27]

However, the reality of the party's position behind this success was very different. In fact the initial campaign had revealed three distinct positions within the ILP. First, the Parliamentary Group and consequently the inner executive and NAC, supported by the many pacifists (and pacificists) within the ILP, advocated a position that the working class should not take sides in the dispute between the 'two rival dictators' in Abyssinia and Italy. They declared that 'the difference between them…[was] not worth the loss of a single British life' and called for the working class to show in every way possible 'their determination that they are not going into another blood bath under the false cry of a small defenceless nation'.[28] Second, in contrast to the neutrality of the Parliamentary Group, the RPC chairman Dr Cullen convinced a majority of the committee to support Abyssinia by working through the League of Nations. Cullen believed that the League had been fundamentally transformed in 1934 when the Soviet Union joined. In his view this meant that the League could be used as 'a stalking horse by the workers'. Thus, he endorsed the Comintern's support for League of Nations sanctions, including military sanctions. He also followed the broader communist popular front line in arguing for a cross-class, anti-fascist, anti-war alliance based on a 'limited and temporary community of interests amongst the general mass of the population including the middle classes'.[29]

Finally, a substantial section of the party including Jack Gaster and Hilda Vernon of the RPC, C.L.R. James of the Marxist Group and Brockway from the ILP leadership, supported a 'workers' sanctions' position. This view, which was also the official line of the ILP's sister parties in the International Bureau of Revolutionary Socialist Unity, differed from the NAC position by indicating that there was an important difference between Abyssinia and Italy, in that Italian action was imperialist. However, they also argued against the popular front line supported by Cullen and against the League of Nations. Particularly central to the workers' sanctions position was the idea that opposition to Italian aggression, if conducted by the workers rather than the League of Nations was also a challenge to British Imperialism.[30] The manoeuvres of those adhering to the different positions as they tried to influence political debate had a number of important consequences in terms of the makeup of the ILP and its relationship with other organisations. This ultimately affected its ability to respond to the unfolding events of the late 1930s.

One immediate consequence was the sidelining of the Revolutionary Policy Committee and the committee's subsequent decision in October 1935 to opt, *en masse*, to join the CPGB. From its formation in 1932, the RPC had been an influential force within the ILP, arguing for closer links with the CPGB and the Comintern. Within the London division, where it was strongest, the RPC played a crucial or even dominant role. The committee was led by Jack Gaster, solicitor and son of the Rabbi Moses Gaster, head of the British Sephardi community, and Dr Carl Cullen, a medical officer specialising in tuberculosis in Poplar. From 1932 the RPC had secured the election of Jack Gaster as divisional, and effectively RPC, representative on the ILP's NAC. In private there had been differences between the two leading figures about a number of issues, most notably about the nature of the relationship between the RPC and the Comintern.[31] However, the division in the RPC leadership, with Gaster supporting workers' sanctions and Cullen supporting League of Nations sanctions, was the first public split since formation. As Gaster himself acknowledged, this represented a 'crisis in the RPC' and at several committee conferences 'a few "personalities" exchanged together with some real straight from the shoulder hitting'.[32] Further, Cullen's line supporting League of Nations' military sanctions against Italy fell outside what many non-RPC party members considered acceptable.

The widespread criticism of this position was welcomed by the party leadership who were opposed to both the factional activity of the RPC and to the communist position of support for the League of Nations. The inner executive, dominated by those who were most opposed to supporting Abyssinia, decided that Cullen, together with other leading RPCers who followed his line, should be deleted from the national speakers' list.[33]

The split within the RPC came to head at the 1935 summer divisional conference of the London and Southern Counties ILP. The regular agenda was suspended so the conference could be devoted to the Abyssinian crisis. The conflict was played out against a backdrop of a significant Trotskyist presence as well as substantial numbers of those opposed to any form of factional organisation. Jack Gaster moved a motion stressing the necessity of working-class organisation against Italian fascism and all imperialist oppression. The motion was supported by the Trotskyists and John Aplin and opposed by his colleagues in the RPC who moved amendments suggesting the use of the League of Nations machinery. The combined forces of the dissidents within the RPC, the Trotskyists and the supporters of Aplin who opposed group organisation held a large majority at the conference. Workers' sanctions were supported by a five to one majority. This represented a considerable setback for the previously dominant RPC.[34] When the division met again at the end of October, it had become clear to the RPC leadership that the committee could not expect to have its own way on either Abyssinia or any other issue discussed by the division. A combination of mounting anti-factional feeling, a growing Trotskyist presence and continuing divisions within the RPC meant that large swathes of its policy were rejected by the very Division in which its strength was greatest.[35] In response the committee staged a dramatic walkout from the conference followed by a call to 'all revolutionary socialists in the party to follow their example and make application to the Communist Party for membership'.[36]

After the departure of the RPC the ILP was able to agree on the negative aspects of its policy: opposition to war and to the League of Nations and its sanctions.[37] However, this did not resolve the internal disputes. Indeed, the conflict between the parliamentary group championing a neutral position and the supporters of workers' sanctions intensified with major consequences for the ILP. These frustrations were dramatically played out at the ILP 1936 national conference held in Keighley. This conference was the first official opportunity to debate the way in which the party leadership had handled the crisis. Central to the dispute was the way the initial declaration in the *New Leader* in support of Abyssinia had been reversed by first the inner executive and then the NAC. C.L.R. James received support from ILPers across the country and from the divisional councils of London and Lancashire, when he attempted to refer back the NAC report, arguing for the centrality of struggle against imperialism and the need to assist colonial peoples. The argument also received some support from NAC members themselves, most notably from Fenner Brockway, the party general secretary. Few from the conference floor were prepared to support the parliamentary group's position. The MPs were left largely to defend their own actions arguing that 'the only way to fight Imperialism was to smash Imperialist Britain'. When it came to voting, James's reference back of the NAC report was joined by a resolution from Lancashire division council backing the early *New Leader* line and stating that the action of the national council was 'in direct conflict with declared Party policy and a contradiction of Party discipline'. The Lancashire resolution was carried by a substantial majority of seventy to fifty-seven. The reference back was also carried but by a margin of only one vote. It appeared that a considerable victory had been won against the parliamentary group.

This impression was swiftly reversed. Following the day's proceedings the parliamentary group met and decided to continue its opposition to the workers' sanction line despite the conference decision. The next morning Maxton presented the conference with a set of options that many considered unpalatable. Bearing in mind the narrowness of the vote, Maxton asked the conference to reverse its policy—putting the policy to a party plebiscite after three months had elapsed. The alternative was to be the open revolt of the parliamentary group who felt 'unable conscientiously to operate the decision'.

Inevitably, the position of the parliamentary group was met with fierce anger from those who felt that they had won a legitimate victory the previous day, notably the Marxist Group. However, many of those who had supported the sanctions line the previous day, led by Brockway, were not prepared to lose the parliamentary group. Brockway stated that though he supported the decision of the conference he felt it would be 'a bad blow for the Party' if the decision taken the day before involved the loss of the chairman. He urged the delegates to accept the proposal for a plebiscite of the membership for 'the sake of the maintenance of the ILP and its work'. After a heated debate the proposal was carried by ninety-three votes to thirty-nine.

Following the conference, and after extended discussions the NAC decided that the plebiscite should be split into two questions. The first asked whether the ILP should have 'declared against Italy and in favour of Abyssinia by the refusal of war materials to Italy'. The second reversed the question and asked whether the party should 'have refused to back either Italy or Abyssinia and opposed the sending of war materials to either side'. The issues were debated in a special issue of *Controversy* devoted to the question of whether workers should take sides in the struggle between Italy and Abyssinia. Two members of the parliamentary group, Maxton and McGovern argued the case against along with the Birmingham pacifist and Quaker Joseph Southall. The contrary position was put by Fenner Brockway, C.L.R. James and Bob Edwards, a member of the Lancashire NAC. The debate was ill-tempered. C.L.R. James bemoaned the 'waste of ink and paper' in dismissing arguments about British imperial interests. Was there 'any child of five', he wondered, who did not know that Italy was seeking to 'make Abyssinia a colony'? Indeed, it is difficult to identify any new substantive issues that were raised in the discussion.

However, two factors combined in favour of the parliamentary group position. First, by the time of the plebiscite, the immediacy of the crisis had passed. The policy of workers' sanctions may have seemed plausible at the outbreak of the crisis almost a year before the plebiscite. By the Keighley conference in March, however, much of its relevance was diminished, although anger against the parliamentary group was still widespread. By the time of the actual plebiscite in May, Abyssinia's Emperor Haile Salassie had been forced to abdicate, and Mussolini had proclaimed the foundation of a new Roman Empire. It was no longer clear what impact an ILP declaration for workers' sanctions could be expected to have. Second, a declaration for workers' sanctions would split the parliamentary group from the party, a consequence that many of those who might otherwise have supported workers' sanctions wished to avoid at all costs. Given the importance and national status that its MPs continued to afford the party, it is perhaps not surprising that the results of the ballot supported the parliamentary group's position by the considerable majority of 809 to 554.[38]

In terms reminiscent of the debates over fusion with the SDF in 1898, the way in which the parliamentary group had forced the issue indicated much about the real distribution of power within the ILP. The plebiscite was a defeat for those who sought a more interventionist opposition to imperialism across the world and a victory for the pacifist line of the parliamentary group. However, the dubious circumstance of this victory meant that the executive committee and the NAC took on the task of attempting to square the circle—finding a logical justification of the expedient policy reversal from the vote for workers' sanction at Keighley and the rejection of this policy in the plebiscite.[39] The resulting policy sought to do this by giving conditional support to a general policy of workers' sanctions in principle, but suggesting that this would not be applied if the policy assisted British (or other) imperialist interests or if the leadership of the subject people were not of a 'character which will eventually make for the emancipation of the working and peasant populations'.[40]

Fractures and splinters in the Labour and anti-war movements

The Italian invasion of Abyssinia left the 'war' party in the Labour movement greatly strengthened and the anti-war movement considerably weakened. For the 'defencists' in the trade union and Labour leadership such as Dalton and Bevin, Citrine and latterly Attlee, the conference debates of 1934 and 1935 in retrospect marked the point at which they began to shift the movement's foreign policy until it reached the stage of withdrawing opposition to the National Government's re-armament programme in 1937 and subsequently entering into the wartime coalition in 1940. A small minority clung to an anti-war position throughout the period, including the war against Germany. But the majority, in light of events in Manchuria, Austria, Abyssinia and Spain, came to accept the need for armed resistance to fascism both by the working class and by the nation-state, even in the absence of a socialist government. Indeed, for many on the left, support for the struggle against fascism in Spain made them the most consistent advocates of the anti-fascist cause, in contrast to the Labour movement leaders who were compromised by their compliance with the National Government's policy of non-intervention.[41]

For those within the Labour movement who continued to hold pacifist beliefs, alliances were harder to build and sustain after Abyssinia. Although the conflict in Spain might be seen as the obvious event, Ceadel sees the Abyssinian crisis as a crucial watershed for the peace movement, marking the separation of the pacificists from the pacifists.[42] This was true in the Labour movement as elsewhere. For instance, the Women's Co-operative Guild continued to advocate a pacifism born from a combination of maternalist feminism, co-operative internationalism and socialist or Christian socialist beliefs that had seen them traditionally allied with the ILP and the No More War Movement.[43] However, with the decline of the ILP and its shift from pacificism to an advocacy of revolutionary or class struggle, otherwise loyal and even moderate Labour guild pacifists became increasingly isolated within the labour movement. During the Abyssinian crisis, the guild opposed any military action and endorsed a resolution from the Women's International League for Peace and Freedom that questioned the 'distribution of, and access to, the world's natural resources.' Attempting to maintain the unity of movement, the guild sought to win support for a League of Nations strengthened by economic sanctions, but without 'recourse to arms under any circumstances'. As the case for armed collective security grew stronger within the wider Labour movement so the guild retreated more into an absolute pacifist position. Their attitude was symbolised by the praise offered to Lansbury for his sacrifice in resigning as an issue of principle.[44]

On this question the guild's closest allies were no longer to be found within the Labour movement but within peace organisations like the Peace Pledge Union (PPU), of which Lansbury had become one of the leading figures. And like Lansbury and the PPU, some of the guild's policies for avoiding war came close to advocating the appeasement of the 'aggressor nations'. Echoing the International Co-operative Women's Guild appeal to 'Mothers of the World', the Women's Co-operative Guild demanded a World Conference on Territories to recommend the redistribution of raw materials and markets to ensure 'justice and equity for all nations.'

Many on the left had been deeply critical of the imperialist and post-1918 settlement that had benefited the Allies at the expense of Germany and had seen legitimate cause for redress. But by the mid to late 1930s the nature of the political regime in Germany was beyond doubt, and for many this line came too close to accepting Hitler's demands as legitimate.[45] After Abyssinia the unity of the peace movement and the alliance between advocates of collective security, socialist pacificists and pacifists was shattered and virtually impossible to reconstruct. It was hoped that the National Peace Council congress in Leeds in June 1936 would identify some common way forward. But delegates were unable to report agreement between the various shades of opinion present. Some pacifists were particularly critical of trade unions, alleging that they had abandoned their opposition to war and rearmament for the sake of increased employment.[46] The differences with the trade unions were both material and also borne of temperament. Most trade union leaders, with the exception of Bevin and some within the AEU, were focussed on domestic industrial issues and tended to view international affairs as the responsibility of the political side of the movement. They would use their votes to ensure that the party remained respectable and electable and that the policies advocated by the party leadership were adopted but they did not seek to change or formulate those policies themselves.

With the majority on the left accepting the need for armed resistance to fascism, by September 1939 there were no divisions or controversies in the movement comparable to 1914. Pacifists like those in the guild made common cause with the remaining anti-war activists within the ILP or sought otherwise unlikely alliances with 'unreliable' communists or distasteful figures on the right. In the end opposition to war came to be largely confined to individual acts of personal conscience rather than a political mass movement.[47] Although Spain forced many more on the left to finally choose between armed resistance and pacificism, Abyssinia demonstrated the unsustainability of the Labour movement's peace alliance. Ceadel remarks that the triple international crises of 1935 to 1936, Abyssinia, the Rhineland and the Spanish Civil War destroyed 'the long-standing compatibility between pacifism and the needs of the socialist movement'. Any remaining advocates of war resistance, the closest in practice to pacifism, were confined to small groupings in the ILP, the ISP and Trotskyist organisations.[48]

Conclusion

In the wider context of the brutality and tragedy of the Italian invasion of Abyssinia, the effects on the British Labour movement might seem inconsequential. Yet the crisis had important and often overlooked effects on the left in Britain. Within the Labour movement much activity depended on complex alliances whose negotiation entailed many considerations. These included institutional constraints, ideological and policy commitments, personal networks and historical relationships, feelings of mutual trust and distrust and sets of shared basic assumptions. The Abyssinian crisis was important because responses inevitably redrew many of these boundaries. The basic anti-war assumption that had informed the language of so much debate on the left was explicitly challenged by the realities of Abyssinia. The emergence and dominance of a new language about war, as used by Bevin,

Dalton and others, created a new and uncomfortable terrain for the left. The crisis also made evident the tensions that had always existed in the anti-war alliance. Most notably, the CPGB's adoption under Soviet tutelage of a language and set of assumptions similar to those increasingly prevalent in the Labour Party signalled the removal of one important, if never fully trusted, participant in any potential anti-war alliance.

But the crisis disrupted the left in even more fundamental ways, exacerbating tensions between groups whose alliances had previously seemed rooted in wider relationships of mutual trust, institutional support and shared basic assumptions. This can be seen most clearly within the ILP, where personal and political relationships broke down as leading figures sought to impose their will on the wider organisation; the compromise over Abyssinia effectively ruled out pacifist response in subsequent conflicts. The terms on which alliances were renegotiated affected not only the ILP's internal dynamics, but also its relationship with other potential anti-war advocates. By the late 1930s the remaining supporters of pacifism on the British left, for instance those within the Women's Co-operative Guild, did not know where to turn for allies. After Abyssinia the alliances on which the peace movement had been based were shattered, and there appeared little prospect of reconstruction.

Notes

1. For discussion see P. Corthorn, 'The Labour Party and the League of Nations: The Socialist League's role in the sanctions crisis of 1935', *Twentieth Century British History* (2002), pp.62–85.
2. For instance, John Shepherd, in an article dealing directly with the 1935 dispute, 'Labour and the trade unions: Lansbury, Ernest Bevin and the leadership crisis of 1935' in C. Wrigley and J. Shepherd (eds), *On The Move: Essays in labour and transport history presented to Philip Bagwell* (London, 1991) pp.205 and 208, refers explicitly only to the defeat of Lansbury 'and his small band of pacifist supporters', while elsewhere indicating that the arguments of Cripps and others on the left proceeded from a markedly different starting point.
3. For a recent overview see C. Sylvest, 'Interwar internationalism, the British Labour Party and the historiography of international relations', *International Studies Quarterly* (2004), p.48.
4. Martin Ceadel, *Pacifism in Britain 1914–1945* (Oxford, 1980); Martin Ceadel, 'Between the wars: Problems of definition' in Richard Taylor and Nigel Young (eds), *Campaigns for Peace: British peace movements in the twentieth century* (Manchester, 1987); Martin Ceadel, *Semi-Detached Idealists: The British peace movement and international relations, 1854–1945* (Oxford, 2000).
5. Ceadel, *Pacifism in Britain*, p.75.

6. Ceadel, *Semi-Detached Idealists*, pp.302–3, 313–14; Corthorn, 'The Labour Party and the League of Nations', pp.68–9; Shepherd (1991), pp.215–17; TUC, *Conference Report* (1934), p.156.

7. Socialist League, *Report of First Annual Conference*, 1933; *Final Agenda for 2nd Annual Conference*, 1934; Corthorn, 'The Labour Party and the League of Nations', pp.66–8; Labour Party archives (LPA) NEC Minutes, 4 September 1934.

8. *Manchester Guardian*, 11 June 1935; NUR, *Reports & Proceedings*, 1935, AGM, president's address and general secretary's report.

9. TUC, *Conference Report*, 1935, p.349; James Figgins, *Labour Monthly*, October 1935; J. P. M. Millar, 'The Abyssinian question—Don't lose your head', *The Plebs*, January 1936.

10. Corthorn, 'The Labour Party and the League of Nations', pp.73–4, 79–80; *Manchester Guardian*, 10, 13, 16 and 17 September 1935.

11. The CPGB did not, however, believe that the imperialist powers, notably Britain, could be trusted to implement sanctions. Instead, it advocated mass pressure on governments and working-class sanctions, a position not unlike that of the Labour leadership. This stance was seen by many on the left as a prime example of 'opportunism' derived from Soviet self-interest and this was reinforced by the CPGB's misrepresentation of its left-wing critics in the ILP and the Socialist League as pacifist and 'pathetic', even though the policy of direct working-class action was supposedly endorsed by the CPGB itself. See *Daily Worker*, 20 and 24 September 1935 and, for a discussion of the CPGB's policy regarding the League of Nations and Abyssinia, Noreen Branson, *History of the Communist Party of Great Britain 1927–1941* (London, 1985), pp.134–42.

12. Corthorn, 'The Labour Party and the League of Nations', pp.72–81; *Reynold's News*, 22 September 1935; Michael Foot, *Aneurin Bevan. Volume 1: 1897–1945* (London, 1979 edn), p.212.

13. *Manchester Guardian*, 19, 20 and 30 September and 1 October 1935; *Reynolds' News*, 29 September 1935; Simon Burgess, *Stafford Cripps: A political life* (London, 1999), pp.95–6.

14. Shepherd, 'Labour and the trade unions', pp.204–30; Labour Party, *Annual Conference Report* (1935), pp.153–93; *Manchester Guardian*, 2 and 3 October 1935; Bernard Donoughue and George Jones, *Herbert Morrison: Portrait of a politician* (London, 2001), pp.235–6.

15. Labour Party, *Annual Conference Report*, 1935, pp.153–93; Burgess, *Cripps*, pp.97–9; *Manchester Guardian*, 2 and 3 October 1935; *Railway Review*, 11 October 1935.

16. For further details on the ISP see G. Cohen 'The Independent Socialist Party' in Keith Gildart, David Howell and Neville Kirk (eds), *Dictionary of Labour Biography. Volume 11* (Aldershot, 2003).

17. For background information on Stockport's political and trade union composition and electoral history, 'The Records of the Stockport Labour Party, 1896–1951. An Introduction' by D. Howell on EP Microfilms; *Manchester*

Guardian, 19 June 1934; Stockport NUR 3 branch resolution calling upon union members 'to refuse to handle war materials for Italy and if necessary, resort to strike action'; NUR *Reports and Proceedings*, 1935, September and December executive committee meetings.

18. *Manchester Guardian*, 19 and 21 September 1935; Stockport Labour Party minutes, 19 September and 28 November 1935; Labour Party, *Annual Conference Report* (1935); LPA NEC Election Sub-Committee, 16 October 1935.
19. *Manchester Guardian*, 12 October 1935.
20. AEU *Monthly Journal*, October 1935.
21. *New Leader*, 15 February 1935.
22. *New Leader*, 13 September 1935.
23. *New Leader*, 18 October 1935.
24. *New Leader*, 9, 13, 20 and 27 September and 11 October 1935.
25. *Controversy*, October 1935.
26. *New Leader*, 4 October 1935.
27. *Forward*, 21 September 1935.
28. *New Leader*, 13 September 1935.
29. C.K.C., 'The War Crisis', *RPC Bulletin*, October 1935.
30. Jack Gaster and the London Emergency Committee, 'Abyssinia—Where does the I.L.P. stand', *Controversy*, October 1935.
31. G. Cohen, 'From "insufferable petty bourgeois" to trusted Communist: Jack Gaster, the Revolutionary Policy Committee and the Communist Party' in J. McIlroy, K. Morgan and A. Campbell (eds), *Party People, Communist Lives* (London, 2001).
32. 'Foreword—crisis in the RPC?', *RPC Bulletin*, October 1935.
33. ILP inner executive minutes, 24 October 1935.
34. *New Leader*, 4 October 1935; Martin Upham, 'The History of British Trotskyism to 1949' (Hull, PhD, 1980) pp.103–4.
35. *New Leader*, 1 November 1935.
36. Upham, 'History of British Trotskyism', p. 104; *RPC Bulletin*, November 1935.
37. Prior to the ILP's 1936 Keighley conference, 48,000 leaflets to this effect signed by the chairman and secretary were distributed to branches and the general public (NAC report, 1936).
38. 3,751 ballot papers were sent out, 1442 were returned (38%), of which eighteen were spoiled. To the first question, 'should the I.L.P. have taken sides with Abyssinia by refusing war materials to Italy', the results were Yes—576 (40%); No—734 (51%). To the second question, 'should the I.L.P. have remained neutral', the results were Yes—809 (56%); No—554 (38%). 660 (46%) of the papers answered yes to question two and no to question one (consistent support for the neutrality position). 462 (32% of the papers answered yes to question one and no to question two (consistent support for the workers' sanctions position); ILP executive committee minutes, 23 May 1936.
39. *United Policy against War: Important NAC Decision Following Plebiscite*, n.d.; NAC report, 1937.

40. ILP, *Through the Class Struggle to Socialism* (London, 1937).

41. Foot, *Bevan*, pp.213*n*. and 220–38 is one account of the Edinburgh Labour Party conference of 1936 in which the left upholds anti-fascist solidarity in the face of the betrayal of Spain by the right.

42. Ceadel, 'Between the wars', pp.88–9.

43. For a more detailed discussion of the Women's Co-operative Guild and the peace movement see Jill Liddington, *The Long Road to Greenham—Feminism and anti-militarism in Britain since 1820* (London, 1989); Gillian Scott, *Feminism and the politics of working women* (Brighton, 1998); Andrew Flinn, 'Prospects for Socialism: the character and implantation of working-class activism in the Manchester area, 1933–1941' (PhD, Manchester 1999).

44. Women's Co-operative Guild Central Committee minutes 7–8 October 1935 and 22 January 1936, Women's Co-operative Guild *Annual Report*, 1936, and *Women's Outlook* October 1935.

45. ICWG Resolution on Peace & the League of Nations November 1935 (DCX/8/1) and Women's Co-operative Guild, *Annual Report* 1936.

46. *Women's Outlook*, 25 July and 8 August 1936.

47. Ceadel, *Semi-Detached Idealists*, pp.389–403.

48. Ceadel, *Pacifism in Britain*, pp.193–5.

A Faraway Country
Abyssinia and the British general election of 1935

David Howell

The British general election of 1935 was held on 14 November, six weeks after Mussolini's troops invaded Abyssinia. Inevitably, the conflict and the appropriate British response featured prominently in the campaign. Such prominence of an international crisis was unique in a twentieth-century British election. Yet what was the significance of the conflict for the result? The complexities can be approached through a more familiar example.

Throughout the 2005 election campaign politicians and commentators debated the impact of the invasion of Iraq. Some dismissed claims about the conflict's significance as a characteristic obsession of liberal and vocal chatterers. But on the doorstep amongst former Labour voters, there was evidence of hostility and uncertainty. The complex pattern of results provided a kaleidoscopic climax to a great campaign. A few declarations provided stark statements. George Galloway's victory on the Respect ticket over the Blairite Oona King in Bethnal Green and Bow could be claimed unequivocally as an anti-war triumph. Together with strong votes for Respect in two other east London seats and in Birmingham Sparkbrook, this success suggested that in some circumstances ethnic solidarities could be mobilised behind an anti-war candidate.

Elsewhere, anti-war sentiment favoured the Liberal Democrats. Their party's position on Iraq was stripped of past ambiguities and effectively presented as anti-war. Although the Liberal Democrats might have predicted significant advances in Tory territory, their balance there was negative, three gains and five losses. In contrast, there were twelve gains from Labour. Some of these seats included amongst their electorates large numbers of students, academics and other sections of the liberally inclined middle class. If the Liberal Democrat policy on student fees was attractive in such constituencies, the party's image on the war might also have made its contribution to some unexpected gains. Although this Liberal Democrat advance at Labour's expense occurred within a relatively narrow social range, the impressive growth of the Liberal Democrat vote in more traditional Labour seats suggests complexities. In some cases, such increase occurred where ethnic groups could perhaps be mobilised on the war issue, but elsewhere, for example in northeastern England, other explanations may be more credible.

This awareness of complexity is a necessary resource for discussion of the relationship between the Abyssinian crisis and the result of the 1935 election. Across the political changes of seven decades there is one important connecting thread. Blair's Labour Party has lost the sympathy of many within the liberal middle class not just over Iraq, but over a range of libertarian issues. In the autumn of 1935, politicians were concerned to retain or win the support of habitually Liberal voters in a context where organised Liberalism was divided and ran relatively few candidates.

Competing for the new mass electorate

Appreciation of the electoral politics of 1935 should begin with an emphasis on the extent to which for experienced politicians the post-war world was novel, uncertain and potentially dangerous. The expansion of the electorate from 7.7 million in 1910 to almost 21.4 million in 1918 and over 28.8 million in 1929 threatened politicians' electoral understanding. They worried about the preferences and competence of new voters. War, regime changes across much of Europe, the spectre of revolution, post-war economic difficulties; all suggested the need for a reconstruction of the party system. More specifically, many Conservatives and Liberals saw the domestication and containment of labour as essential.[1] The increase in trade union membership in the decade after 1910 and post-war industrial radicalism provided one incentive; the expanded franchise offered another. Trade union membership and radicalism diminished in the 1920s due to depression and defeat, but the Labour Party had become a stronger and durable factor in electoral and parliamentary politics. In the confused election of November 1922, the return of 142 Labour members demonstrated that the party had a firm presence, not amongst the working class as a whole, but within specific occupational groups. Much inter-war party activity and bargaining can be read as a series of attempts to construct an effective response. One consequence was the splintering and marginalisation of the Liberal Party.

The Lloyd George Coalition of 1918–22 responded to democratisation and to post-war economic social and international challenges with an attempt to combine Conservatives and Liberals, perhaps in a new Centre party, that could offer modernisation and resistance to 'dangerous' radicalism. The attempt foundered on depression, deflation and tribal partisanship.[2]

By the autumn of 1924 a second strategy had emerged: an electorally effective Conservative Party under Stanley Baldwin. Its decisive victory in the October 1924 election ended the first brief period of Labour government. Baldwin's party eschewed grand programmes; its leader seemingly personified English virtues and limitations. Yet the party's foot soldiers, and in more elevated cadences Baldwin himself, could also use rough tactics. The 1924 campaign aroused the spectre of Bolshevism in the context of the Russian treaty and the Campbell case to question Labour's fitness for office, mobilising the apathetic and enticing anxious Liberals. The Zinoviev Letter merely provided the coping stone.[3]

This Baldwinite triumph depended on the marginalisation of the Liberal Party. In the 1924 election the Liberals lost 119 seats and almost 1.4 million votes. These lost voters favoured the Conservatives, one authority suggests, by a ratio of 3:2.[4] Yet this Conservative dominance was vulnerable to any Liberal revival that by cutting Tory support could strengthen Labour's parliamentary position. This fear was realised in the 1929 election. The Liberal campaign was vigorous and well funded. It attracted many more votes but produced only a small increase in seats. The principal consequence was to destroy the Conservative majority and make Labour the biggest single party in the Commons for the first time.

	1924 Election		1929 Election	
	%	Seats	%	Seats
Conservative	48.3	419	38.2	260
Liberal	17.6	40	23.4	59
Labour	33.0	151	37.1	288

Labour's second period in office disillusioned many supporters. As unemployment rose, the government's attempts to reconcile the demands of economic orthodoxy with the modest expectations of the Labour movement over unemployment benefit became increasingly contorted. Conservatives quarrelled over the merits of Baldwin's leadership.[5] Liberals increasingly fragmented over the appropriate response to a beleaguered government. By the summer of 1931 by-election results indicated strong backing for the Conservatives yet with the economic and political crisis of August 1931, a new political landscape rapidly emerged.[6]

Following the disintegration of the Labour government, a National Government emerged headed by the former Labour icon Ramsay MacDonald. The government was supported by the Conservatives, by all the

Liberal fragments except for Lloyd George and his family, and by a dozen former Labour members. The combination was widely expected to be temporary; no element wished to court the political peril of sole responsibility for extensive cuts in public expenditure. However, the rapid and decisive October 1931 election gave the government the most massive of majorities. Labour was almost extinguished, dependent for parliamentary survival on most coalfields and east London. Whilst the new House of Commons was overwhelmingly Conservative, the government's composition continued to demonstrate its 'National' aspirations, and to signpost a well-founded belief that this victory depended on far more than the established Conservative vote.[7]

1931 Election					
National Government	**%**	**Seats**	**Opposition**	**%**	**Seats**
Conservative	55.0	471	Labour	30.7	52
National Labour	1.6	12	Lloyd George Liberal	0.5	4
Liberal National	3.7	35			
Liberal	6.5	33			
National	0.3	3			
Total	**67.1**	**554**		**31.2**	**56**

Notes

1. Liberal Nationals under Sir John Simon co-ordinated their electoral efforts with the Conservatives. Only four Liberal Nationals faced Conservative opponents. In contrast, eighty-one Liberals under the leadership of Sir Herbert Samuel faced Conservative opposition.
2. The fifty-two Labour Members included forty-six officially endorsed, five Independent Labour Party and one Independent (Josiah Wedgwood).

This outcome provided the baseline for the electoral calculations that preceded the 1935 contest. Two considerations should be emphasised. First, there was a belief in the continuing significance of the Liberal vote that had so affected outcomes in successive elections. Second, on the basis of results since 1922, general elections had typically seen large numbers of seats changing hands. Therefore, the inference could be made that the 1931 landslide should not be relied on as a guarantee of long-term governmental security.

Inevitably, given the underlying resilience of its electoral support, the Labour Party demonstrated a significant recovery in by-elections. Between March 1932 and July 1935 the party fought eleven seats that it had lost in 1931. It regained eight of them. In every case but one, Labour polled a higher percentage than at any previous election.[8] Although the party also achieved some massive swings in safer government seats, only two further gains resulted. One, Liverpool Wavertree in February 1935, was the result of a split Conservative vote. An earlier success, East Fulham, in October 1933, has produced political and historiographical controversy. Baldwin claimed subsequently that the turnaround of votes was attributable to a pacifist Labour campaign, and therefore led to government caution on rearmament. East Fulham was one of a cluster of contests in autumn 1933 where Labour candidates emphasised a conciliatory approach to international affairs and rejected realpolitik and rearmament. Their candidates often scored strong votes in apparently unpromising areas. However, close examination of the East Fulham contest has suggested the significance of high rents and overcrowding. The following year Labour gained control of Fulham borough council for the first time since 1919, presumably on rents rather than opposition to rearmament.[9]

Labour would obviously recover from the depth of October 1931 in any future election. Nevertheless, economic depression meant financial problems; often local organisation was weak. Post-mortems on the 1931 disaster and the preceding problems in office led to disputes, moderated to some degree by the convenient availability of National Government renegades as scapegoats. The circumstances of the debacle had promoted a search for an effective concordat between politicians and trade union leaders. By mid-1935 the party had made significant advances electorally and programmatically, not least the capture of the London County Council in autumn 1934. But one major obstacle had to be addressed. In 1931 Labour's parliamentary presence had been virtually destroyed despite winning 30.7 per cent of the vote, the result of facing a united opposition for the first time. Its adversaries, irrespective of party label, had attracted much of the Liberal vote. Labour hopes depended on some fragmentation of the National bloc, or at least a drift of Liberal sympathisers to the Labour Party.

The Liberal Party after 1931 provided a chronicle of disputes and disasters.[10] Lloyd George remained estranged from the section led by Sir Herbert Samuel. The differences between the sections led by Samuel and Sir John Simon were never resolved. Several Liberal members were initially unclear as to their allegiance, and in some cases would have preferred to have avoided a decision. However, the government's introduction of tariffs in 1932 initially forced the choice. After all, for many Liberals Free Trade was the most fundamental element in their identity. Samuel and his colleagues initially withdrew from the government in September 1932. Only in November 1933 did he and twenty-nine colleagues cross the floor into formal opposition. Such a protracted odyssey did not impress the electorate. The Samuelites' electoral record in 1932 had been credible, but following the shift into opposition interventions were limited by financial stringency.[11] Often candidates found difficulty in articulating a clear identity. Occasional promising results, for example at Basingstoke in April 1934, were overshadowed by cases of declining support and failures to contest. The nadir came in October 1934 following the death of the popular Liberal member for North Lambeth. His successor as Liberal candidate was trounced by his Labour opponents. The Samuelites were squeezed between Sir John Simon's group, represented at every level of the government and insisting on their Liberal pedigree, and on the other side Lloyd George with his Council of Action. Lloyd George disparaged Samuelite credibility and sought to endorse progressives whatever their formal political label. The shambles that was Liberalism strengthened the belief in other parties that the fate of the Liberal vote would be crucial.

This situation could be expected to strengthen Conservative optimism. The National appeal had attracted Liberals in 1931; Sir John Simon's group subsequently became even closer to the Conservatives. However, Conservatives experienced significant internal dissent. There was a widespread, if exaggerated belief that the extent of the party's benevolence at the 1931 election had not been appreciated by other smaller pro-government elements. Conservatives often presented themselves as having foregone a certain party victory in the national interest. They pointed with increasing asperity to the limitations of a National Labour prime minister and a Liberal National foreign secretary, playing down the achievement of tariffs.[12] The Conservative right forcefully opposed the government's India policy, opening up the possibility of a rift between true conservatism and the policies of the National Government. Concern developed, as it had during the Lloyd George coalition, that involvement in the National Government would dilute party identity as propaganda would be National rather than Conservative.[13]

Gradually the difficulties eased. The imminent passing of the India legislation effectively terminated that divisive controversy. Cabinet changes in June 1935 brought Baldwin back to the premiership in place of MacDonald. Simon's record at the Foreign Office had been widely criticised. He was replaced by Sir Samuel Hoare, an ambitious and flexible Conservative who had piloted the deeply controversial India bill through the Commons.[14] Overall, the government became more Conservative, but its Liberal National and National Labour allies had nowhere else to go. It remained to be seen whether this assessment of their options was shared widely amongst those who had backed the government in 1931.

Ministers could point to economic recovery from the crisis of 1931. Unemployment had fallen, but the revival was geographically and occupationally uneven. Nevertheless, the government could claim to be a safer option than the Labour Party that had presided over rising unemployment and had failed to cope with a financial crisis. The National Government's economic policies lacked the vigour and vision of the American New Deal, but on balance they were probably an electoral asset by mid-1935.

Abyssinia and the election

Electoral considerations were challenged by the escalation of the Abyssinia crisis. Italian ambitions towards Abyssinia were longstanding. The frontier clash at Walwal late in 1934 precipitated what proved to be the decisive crisis. The British cabinet only began to discuss the question as a matter of urgency in mid-1935. The key Ministers were all Conservatives—Baldwin, Hoare and the minister for the League of Nations, Anthony Eden.[15] In addition, the Chancellor of the Exchequer, Neville Chamberlain, was the most powerful member of the cabinet.

Increasingly concerned with the policies and pretensions of Nazi Germany, ministers viewed Italy as a potentially significant partner in any attempt to restrain German ambitions. Britain, France and Italy had come together at Stresa in the spring of 1935. For many British Conservatives and Foreign Office officials the fascist character of Mussolini's regime was not an issue. Some empathised with its liquidation of the left or admired its self-consciously energetic style.[16] Others simply saw the character of the Italian regime as irrelevant in the context of European security. Moreover, British ministers saw African acres as bargainable in a bid to prevent conflict between European states. In June 1935, the cabinet approved a deal whereby the British would transfer the Red Sea port of Zeila to Abyssinia in return for Abyssinian territorial concessions to Italy. Eden, popularly viewed as the prime supporter of the League of Nations within the government, took details of the deal to Rome. His journey ended with Italian rejection.

The Baldwin government's attempts to manage the crisis were complicated by Abyssinia's membership of the League of Nations. This dated back to 1923, when Abyssinian membership had been achieved with Italian support and against British and French opposition. Following the Walwal incident, Abyssinia appealed to the League. The question of Britain's commitment to the League became electorally more sensitive in late June, immediately after Italian rejection of the British plan for a territorial exchange. The League of Nations Union announced the results of its misleadingly named Peace Ballot. Over eleven and a half million people participated, and ten million endorsed economic and other non-military sanctions against an aggressor. Military sanctions were supported by more than six and three-quarter million, a significant decrease, although over two and a half times the number who opposed this escalation. However loaded the questions, the ballot represented an expression of support for collective security that no government in a pre-election period could ignore. Participants doubtless included many of liberal sentiments who had voted for the National Government in 1931, but who might be less inclined to repeat this support should government policy threaten to damage the League's credibility.

Prior to Baldwin's return to the premiership, the cabinet had explored the possibility of a rapprochement with Lloyd George. Such an arrangement could refurbish the government's claim to be National and retain Liberal support. However, Neville Chamberlain's opposition proved decisive.[17] Instead, Baldwin as prime minister attempted to use the result of the Peace Ballot and anxieties over Abyssinia to appeal to the liberally inclined. He emphasised the government's commitment to the League and used the crisis to justify rearmament. This could be presented to those suspicious of ministerial intentions as a contribution to collective security, and not a return to a policy that for many had resulted in the calamity of 1914.

The strategy had ambiguities and silences. Popular sympathy for Abyssinia and support for the League could be mobilised to endorse rearmament, not so much against Italy or as a contribution to collective security, but for defence against Germany. The extent of any rearmament programme was obscure. Rhetoric in support of the League was more prominent than doubts about its effectiveness and in particular about the reliability of the French. Rhetoric and ambiguities served to mask differences within the cabinet over the extent to which the League should be backed, and diverse views amongst government backbenchers about how far this approach jeopardised British interests in the eastern Mediterranean and East Africa.[18]

The Government's pro-League rhetoric was presented by Hoare to the League of Nations Assembly on 11 September. Britain would stand by its obligations to the League. Domestic Labour and Liberal critics were wrong-footed. At the start of October, government electoral prospects were boosted when George Lansbury, the Labour Party's pacifist leader, resigned following his savaging by the Transport Workers' leader Ernest Bevin at the party's annual conference. The drama of the occasion was heightened by the imminence of Italian military action. The outcome of the debate, strong support for the League including in the last resort military sanctions, was predictable. This had been the position of the Trades Union Congress the previous month; in the party forum union votes replicated this decision. The destruction of Lansbury and the accompanying anti-intellectual denigration of Sir Stafford Cripps were trade union affirmations of the acceptable post-1931 relationship between themselves and the political leadership. In a pre-election context the fracas and the replacement of Lansbury by an apparent locum, Attlee, only served to diminish Labour's credibility.[19]

There remained concern amongst the government's critics that ministerial sermons about the League could well be for electoral purposes only. Late in October MPs debated the Abyssinian situation. Dai Grenfell, a South Wales miners' MP hinted, 'if there is a deal, I predict that deal will be after the election'.[20] A more thorough and prescient claim was presented by Eleanor Rathbone, the Independent (progressive and feminist) member for the Combined English Universities:

> The public realise that in the Cabinet there are two parties, one which really believes and trusts in the League, and one which disbelieves in it and regards it as a sentimental delusion which can be turned to good account as a means of persuading the electorate to consent to great increases of armaments. I would appeal to the right honourable Gentleman [Hoare] to remember that large numbers of people, hundreds of thousands, possibly millions, are going in the next few weeks to vote for the present Government, largely because they believe that they are voting for the party of the right honourable Gentleman and for his colleague, the Member for the League of Nations [Eden]. If they should find afterwards that the policy of the Government that is to be—the Government that will no doubt issue out of the election—is, in fact, not the policy of the right honourable Gentleman but the policy of the other faction in the Cabinet, there will be bitter disillusion and a sense of betrayal which will visit itself upon the whole of the Government.[21]

Such doubts were hardly quelled by Baldwin's response. Alongside his affirmation of 'absolute loyalty to the Covenant', he mentioned the need to consider 'any legitimate opportunity for a settlement'. He acknowledged that critics might characterise this as 'a loophole for going behind the back of the League of Nations'. His reassurance was bizarre. Any settlement 'must be one fair alike to the three parties, Italy, Abyssinia…and to the League of Nations itself'.[22] For Baldwin the burglar, the householder and the police, all merited proper consideration.

Whatever the weaknesses in the government's position and the reservations, often suppressed, of those who stood as its candidates, the result of the election was an overwhelming victory for the government.

1935 Election					
National Government	%	Seats	Opposition	%	Seats
Conservative	47.7	387	Labour	37.8	154
National Labour	1.6	8	Liberals	6.5	20
Liberal National	4.0	33			
National	0.4	3			
Totals	53.7	431		44.3	174

Notes
1. The Opposition also included five more members who were firmly on the left: four Independent Labour Party members from Glasgow and one communist, Willie Gallacher, representing West Fife. All five of these constituencies had returned Labour members prior to 1931.
2. All tables exclude Irish Nationalists, one in 1924, three in 1929, two in 1931 and two in 1935. They should be seen as anti-Conservative.

Aftermath

A Conservative sceptic, Leo Amery, had suppressed much of his concern about Baldwin's policy: 'It seemed that the whole thing figured in his mind as a useful aid to winning the election, and that he had no idea of its repercussions outside.'[23] These became evident within weeks of Baldwin's triumph. The result was to confirm Eleanor Rathbone's expectations and to devastate the post-election optimism of government backbenchers. Negotiations between Hoare and the French premier Pierre Laval would have given Mussolini a large portion of Abyssinia in return for Britain making available a vulnerable Abyssinian access to the sea. This was dismissed by *The Times* as a 'corridor for camels'.[24] The extent of wider ministerial complicity in the deal remains predictably unclear. Earlier attempts to support foundered on backbench hostility, and the cabinet decided, eight days after the leaking of the proposals, that he should be asked to resign. The mood on the government benches was noted by Brendan Bracken, reporting to his absent mentor Winston Churchill:

> The general feeling running through the whole House is that Hoare has let the country down with a resounding bang…Baldwin, who was on a pinnacle three or four days ago, is now greatly discredited. The Liberals and nonconformists whose language he speaks and whose support of the Conservative Party is said to be due to Baldwin's personality and character will never forgive him.[25]

Criticism amongst Government backbenchers was significantly reduced by Hoare's temporary sacrifice of office. Baldwin's two commons speeches on the crisis were inadequate, but talk of a threat to the government's survival, barely a month after a major electoral triumph was clearly absurd. Cripps might indict the government, many of its backbenchers might feel uneasy, but a majority of over 250, however discredited the strategy, was immovable:

> The Prime Minister, with an astuteness which marks his political leadership, realised that the peace sentiment might be used electorally by the National Government, provided that for a time, it was made to appear to the people that the Liberal sentiment was in the ascendancy in the Government. The true Imperialist basis of their policy was soft-pedalled very gently while the Liberal sentiment were blared from every platform all over the country.[26]

The shocked reaction of many government backbenchers to the Hoare-Laval Pact followed by the dropping of the Foreign Secretary suggested that for many successful candidates, the policy of support for collective security was important, and was reckoned to have affected the election result. Therefore, the belief developed that the government's majority was the result of a fraudulent policy that was jettisoned, albeit in disorderly fashion, once the election was won. Such an assessment fails to do justice to the complexities of the international situation. Moreover, closer inspection of the election results should perhaps encourage scepticism about this verdict.

One possibility had been ruled out before polling day. There was no serious risk of widespread loss of government supporters to opposition Liberal candidates. There were too few, only 159. The question of the Liberal vote in most constituencies resolved itself into three choices, National Government, Labour or abstention. There is some evidence of abstention in specific seats but generally in straight fights, the government retained the majority of Liberal sympathisers. Labour's share of the poll was actually higher than in 1929, but it won over 130 fewer seats.[27]

Labour's gains were also geographically and occupationally limited. It regained some presence in several cities from which it had been evicted in 1931, although not in Newcastle, Salford, Birmingham, Leicester and Cardiff. In cities where it had hung on in 1931 it expanded;[28] in the coal-fields, it deepened its majorities and regained lost seats in Durham. Above all, compared with 1931, Labour was twenty-five seats stronger in the London area. But outside the capital, the southern half of England proved a disaster. Apart from two Bristol seats and the Forest of Dean, Labour's 'southern English' provincial outposts were Nuneaton and Nottingham. There were also failures in northern constituencies characterised by signif-icant trade unionism and economic depression. Only three gains were made in the cotton towns.

Labour was successful only in seats dominated by the industrial working class. The only clear exception was the unexpected victory in the Gaelic speaking Western Isles; also heavily Welsh-speaking Carmarthen had high concentrations of both agricultural workers and coal miners. However, Labour's successes cannot be explained simply in class terms. Its victories came in some cities and amongst some occupational groups. Its electoral position was complex, reflecting the varied experiences, memories and pri-orities of occupations and communities and also diversity in the pattern of party competition. Labour candidates performed exceptionally well against Liberal National and above all National Labour incumbents who had per-haps enjoyed an electoral bonus in 1931.[29]

This anatomy of Labour support suggests that very little is explicable by reference to the Abyssinia crisis. Explanations should focus on the diversity of economic, community and cultural experiences and expectations, and their relationship to party identities. Scepticism about the electoral signifi-cance of the Abyssinia crisis can be strengthened through an analysis of the Liberal performance. Where former Liberal voters who had gone National in 1931 had the choice of voting Liberal, they were often reluctant to do so. This could suggest that potential Liberal supporters were sticking to their 1931 choice because of the government's advocacy of collective security. However, this hypothesis, in reflecting the character of much contemporary political debate, arguably misunderstands the bases for Liberal support in the

1930s, and arguably for some years before.

The Liberals won nineteen geographical seats plus the University of Wales.[30] Of the geographical successes, six were in Wales; four of them, the Lloyd George family party. All six seats were predominantly rural and had high numbers of Welsh speakers. In each case the Liberals had been long established as the representative of a culture, a way of life. Ten of the Liberal victories were in England. Five were rural, one each in Devon and Cornwall, two bordering Scotland and one in the Fens.[31] All had majorities of fewer than one thousand. None had a Labour candidate. They were highly vulnerable. Five urban seats returned Liberal members; in two cases without Conservative opposition.[32] The remaining three seats were Scottish. Two urban members in Dundee and Paisley had benefited from the lack of a Conservative opponent.[33] In the far north the Liberal Member for Caithness and Sutherland was Sir Archibald Sinclair, who owned 100,000 acres in his constituency. After the 1935 election he became leader of what remained of independent Liberalism. Liberal successes were not the result of the impact of national debates about collective security, Abyssinia and Mussolini's aggressive intentions. Rather, they reflected the capacity of candidates to present themselves as effective representatives of local identities and interests whilst sealing off local political debates from the dominant National Government-Labour dichotomy.

Baldwin's electoral triumph in November 1935 owed little to Abyssinia as a substantive issue. Rather, his ambiguous advocacy of collective security strengthened the government's and especially the Conservative Party's ability to develop affinities between its sentiments and symbols, and the concerns, prejudices and taboos of many electors. The party settlement arrived at as a rapid response to crisis in 1931 had survived despite internal tensions and external shocks. Its durability was apparent as the international outlook deteriorated—the Rhineland, Spain, Austria, the dismemberment of Czechoslovakia. Avuncular Baldwin gave way to acerbic Neville Chamberlain. If Hitler's armies had not invaded Poland, a peacetime election would have returned Chamberlain with a sizeable majority. The success of 1935 would in all probability have had its sequel in 1940. Instead, there came military disaster, 'Guilty Men' and the Churchillian myth of the 1930s.[34] The bases for the National Government's dominance were far more rooted than short-term electoral trickery and were best forgotten by all concerned.

Stanley Baldwin's confidant Tom Jones, reflected on the 1935 campaign:

> The triumph is a personal one for S.B. Over all he has thrown that halo of faith and hope, free from meretricious ornament, which inspires con-

fidence. The effect is to gather to the help of the Tories a large voting strength of Liberals and unattached folk who like his sober and sincere accents and who are afraid of the menace to small owners and investors associated with socialism.[35]

In a radio broadcast in September 1938 Neville Chamberlain characterised Czechoslovakia as 'a faraway country'.[36] In the 1930s it was not the only one. It has a contemporary successor.

Notes

1. Maurice Cowling, *The Impact of Labour, 1920–1924* (Cambridge, 1971) offers a rich analysis of politicians' responses. He extends the analysis in *The Impact of Hitler: British politics and British policy, 1933–1940* (Cambridge, 1975).
2. See Kenneth O. Morgan, *Consensus and Disunity: the Lloyd George Coalition Government, 1918–1922* (Oxford, 1979).
3. The best analysis of Baldwin's politics is Philip Williamson, *Stanley Baldwin* (Cambridge, 1999). See also the study by Stuart Ball in *Oxford Dictionary of National Biography*, vol.3 (Oxford, 2004).
4. Ross McKibbin, 'Class and conventional wisdom: the Conservative Party and the "public" in interwar Britain' in McKibbin, *The Ideologies of Class: Social relations in Britain, 1880–1950* (Oxford, 1990), pp.259–93.
5. See Stuart Ball, *Baldwin and the Conservative Party* (New Haven, CT, 1988).
6. See Philip Williamson, *National Crisis and National Government: British politics, the economy and empire, 1926–1932* (Cambridge, 1992).
7. Andrew Thorpe, *The British General Election of 1931* (Oxford, 1991). See also John Fair, 'The Conservative basis for the formation of the National Government in 1931', *Journal of British Studies*, 1980, pp.142–64; D.H. Close, 'The realignment of the electorate in 1931', *History*, 1982, pp.393–404.
8. Seats gained—Wakefield, Wednesbury, Rotherham, Hammersmith North, West Ham, Upton, Lambeth North, Swindon, Liverpool West Toxteth. Only Swindon was lost again in 1935. Hammersmith was the only case where the Labour percentage of the poll fell (just) below 1929. This was attributable to a communist intervention.
   Seats not regained—Dunbartonshire, Kilmarnock, Edinburgh West. Too much should not be made of the Anglo-Scottish distinction. Dunbartonshire and Edinburgh West had been narrow victories in 1929, Labour's only one in the latter constituency, Kilmarnock was not regained in November 1933 because of a split vote with the Independent Labour Party.
9. See Richard Heller, 'East Fulham revisited', *Journal of Contemporary History*, 1971, pp.172–96; Tom Stannage, 'The East Fulham by-election, 25 October 1933', *Historical Journal*, 1971, pp.165–200.
10. For material see Bernard Wasserstein, *Sir Herbert Samuel: A political life* (Oxford,

1992); David Dutton, *Simon: A political biography of Sir John Simon* (London, 1992); for a recent summary of key themes see David Dutton, '1932: a neglected date in the history of the Liberal Party', *Twentieth Century British History*, 2003, pp.43–60.

11. During 1932 Liberals had polled credibly in the absence of Labour candidates at Henley in February and Dulwich in June. They had retained the marginal North Cornwall seat in July and the much safer Cardiganshire in September.

12. For the decline of Ramsay MacDonald see David Marquand, *Ramsay MacDonald* (London, 1977), chs 27–30.

13. For a summary of Conservative problems see Tom Stannage, *Baldwin Thwarts the Opposition: the British general election of 1935* (London, 1980), ch.1.

14. See J. A. Cross, *Sir Samuel Hoare: A political biography* (London, 1977).

15. Eden's career, not least his attitude to the League of Nations, remains controversial. See Robert Rhodes James, *Anthony Eden* (London, 1986), ch.5; David Dutton, *Anthony Eden: A life and reputation* (London, 1997), ch.2; D. R. Thorpe, *Eden: The life and times of Anthony Eden* (London, 2003), ch.6.

16. For example, Winston Churchill's praise of Mussolini in 1927, cited in Martin Gilbert, *Prophet of Truth: Winston S. Churchill, 1922–1939* (London, 1990); and from the Labour side, the case of Hugh Dalton in 1932, for which see Ben Pimlott, *Hugh Dalton* (London, 1985), pp.213–15.

17. Chamberlain's antagonism to Lloyd George dated back to his brief and unhappy period as Director-General of National Service in 1917.

18. For a nuanced analysis of Baldwin's strategy see Williamson, *Stanley Baldwin*, pp.50–2, 310–12. Material on Conservative attitudes can be found in Neville Thompson, *The Anti-Appeasers: Conservative opposition to appeasement in the 1930s* (Oxford, 1971), ch.4.

19. For a sympathetic view of Bevin's behaviour see Alan Bullock, *The Life and Times of Ernest Bevin*, vol.1: *Trade Union Leader, 1881–1940* (London, 1960), pp.560–71; for a less positive assessment, Peter Weiler, *Ernest Bevin* (Manchester, 1993), pp.86–93. For Lansbury see John Shepherd, *George Lansbury: At the heart of old Labour* (Oxford, 2002), ch.16; for Cripps in the context of his post-1931 politics, Peter Clarke, *The Cripps Version: The life of Sir Richard Stafford Cripps* (London, 2002), pp.52–67. For the debate on 1–2 October 1935, see *Labour Party Conference Report*, 1935, pp.153–93.

20. *House of Commons Debates* [HC Deb], 5th series, vol.305, col.139.

21. HC Deb, 5th series, vol.305, col.129. For Rathbone, the Abyssinia cause became a long-term commitment. See Susan Pedersen, *Eleanor Rathbone and the Politics of Conscience* (New Haven and London, 2004), pp.273–6.

22. HC Deb, 5th series, vol.305, col.150.

23. Diary entry for 15 October 1935, in John Barnes and David Nicholson (eds), *The Empire at Bay: The Leo Amery Diaries, 1929–1945* (London, 1988), p.401.

24. *The Times*, 16 December 1935.

25. Brendan Bracken to Winston Churchill, 11 December 1935, in Martin Gilbert (ed.), *Winston S. Churchill*, vol.V companion, 1929–1935 (London, 1981), p.1349.

26. HC Deb, 5th series, vol.307, col.2065.

27. For analysis of the results see Stannage, *Baldwin Thwarts the Opposition*, ch.9 and appendix 1.

28. Labour gained four seats in Manchester and four in Sheffield, three in Stoke, two in Hull and one in Aberdeen, Edinburgh, Bradford and Nottingham. It increased its holdings from two to five in Glasgow, one to three in Liverpool, one to two in Leeds and Bristol. In addition, four Glasgow seats were won by members of the Independent Labour Party.

29. The ultimate example was Ramsay MacDonald at Seaham; see Marquand, *Ramsay MacDonald*, pp.779–81.

30. Some sources give twenty-one as the overall total. They include R. D. Bernays [Bristol North]. He did not cross into opposition in November 1933, but only took the National Liberal whip in 1936.

31. Barnstaple, North Cornwall, Berwick on Tweed, North Cumberland and Isle of Ely.

32. Bethnall Green South West and Bradford South (no Conservative opponent), Birkenhead East, Middlesbrough West and Wolverhampton East (three cornered).

33. The Paisley Liberal candidate stood as 'a liberal candidate prepared to support the government on all lines of progressive policy consistent with Liberal principles'; cited in Catriona M. M. Mcdonald, *The Radical Thread, Political Change in Scotland: Paisley politics, 1885–1924* (East Linton, 2000), p.272.

34. *Guilty Men* was the title of a polemic published in the summer of 1940 that attacked the political leadership of MacDonald, Baldwin, Neville Chamberlain and their acolytes. Written by three Beaverbrook journalists, Michael Foot, Peter Howard and Frank Owen, it was published under the pseudonym Cato.

35. Tom Jones to Abraham Flexner (Princeton), 17 November 1935, in Thomas Jones, *A Diary with Letters, 1930–1950* (London, 1954), pp.155–6.

36. The broadcast was on the evening of 27 September 1938, before Chamberlain's third meeting with Hitler at Munich and when hopes of avoiding war seemed to be diminishing; see *The Times*, 28 September 1938.

Forum

Who Will Design Lenin's New Suit?
The 2005 Moscow Biennale

Margarita Tupitsyn

'*Maybe we have to juxtapose the ghost of Lenin with the ghost of Christian Dior!*'[1]

Once upon a time.

After the collapse of the USSR in 1991, many examples of Soviet monumental propaganda were removed. Notorious institutions either acquired new names or closed down altogether. The Lenin Mausoleum, however, was curiously spared. It did not, for example, suffer the fate of the monument to the first KGB chief Felix Dzerzhinsky. Safe from the indifferent mob, the mausoleum continues to receive support from a government committed to preserve not only Aleksei Shchusev's emblematic and unarguably successful architectural structure,[2] but paradoxically the leader's body.

At the start of this year, the radio station *The Echo of Moscow* (Ekho Moskvy) reported that the mausoleum was closing for several months in order to 'freshen up' Lenin's body which, against the will of his wife, was embalmed eighty years ago. The report summarised that in general Lenin's body was in a 'good shape', and in its present state could carry on for another hundred years. On the other hand, the radio reported, the leader's suit was showing signs of serious deterioration.

Such frank discussion of Lenin's funerary outfit (unthinkable before *perestroika*) throws a bridge from the mausoleum—built in the heart of Red Square—to the location, on the edge of the same square, of the ex-State Lenin Museum that was chosen as the main site of the first Moscow Biennale. Opened in 1936 in the former headquarters of the tsarist Duma—implying, perhaps, that the Soviet state was not to be a legislative society but an autocracy, be it in collective memory (Lenin) or in reality (Stalin)—the building presently stands empty while awaiting its latest role. Before the Lenin Museum was cleared of its exhibits, it included a display of Lenin's worldly possessions, among which was a Rolls Royce (currently displayed near the staff entrance of the adjacent State Historical Museum next to a brand new model) and examples of Lenin's wardrobe—all attesting to the communist leader's good and less than modest taste.

Since the mid-1930s and until its recent demolition, the famous Hotel Moscow (also built by Shchusev) used to be a neighbour of both the mausoleum and the Lenin Museum. Intended to be called Mossovet (after Moscow Council), it eventually adopted the capital's name, and for several decades functioned as a space where Soviet style luxury was mixed with ideological surveillance. The scale of the hotel construction and ideological ambitions of the state as its sponsor, are conveyed in a number of billboards made by Gustav Klutsis during the period of hotel's construction. Equally ambitious is its current *re*-construction. During the opening of the Biennale it was wrapped with huge BVLGARI's adverts, leaving no doubt about the hotel's future ideological orientations. Where Klutsis' montages showed a bodily unity of straitlaced marxist leaders, the image prepared by BVLGARI bluntly defies the representational models and values of the former Soviet regime. On it a couple of alienated females (dispersed to the far left and to the far right) are captured in a tactile relationship with their jewels.

'Accidental Collages'

'Are Russians…Europeans? Or something different? If they are something unique, then they are definitely not something Asian? Or wholly European?'[3]

It is not entirely clear why the international group of curators of the Biennale which presented forty-one artists from all over the world decided to show in the largest room of the former Lenin Museum, Mikhail Romm's 1958 documentary *Lenin is Alive* (Zhivoi Lenin). Does this make Romm a participant in this unprecedented (for Russia) cultural event? Or did the curators want to set up a background for the space they were assigned to use? Was the showing of this film (made by the director from the generation of the Russian avant-garde film-makers) designed to illustrate their collective conviction that 'curators should be skilful editors'? After all no one is more involved in the editorial process than film-makers.

Whatever the reason, it constructed a metaphor that revealed to the Russian viewer that the 'non-accidental iconography' which they had either grown up with or inherited, was being replaced by an image production whose global distribution was most of the time accidental. This was confirmed at the outset of the display of work by the Biennale participants with Paulina Olowska's poignantly titled series 'Accidental Collages'. Olowska made this work after encountering Kazimir Malevich's didactic charts, executed using collage and including some of the multiple images that helped him to explain the genealogy of Suprematism. Although Malevich's charts were originally shown next to Olowska's 'Accidental Collages' at the Stedelijk Museum, they were absent here. Given that Malevich's early modernist status in Russia is exceptional, the inclusion of his charts—even in the form of reproductions—could have prevented this series from coming across as a belated replay of numerous post-modernist collages made throughout the world in the 1980s.

It is hard to know if this was a deliberate act of de-contextualisation or simply what the curators called their own 'laziness'. Nowhere did they provide a key to their selection process (except by saying that they selected emerging artists). Most of the time we did not know who chose whom unless we assumed that a curator's nationality corresponded to the nationality of an artist. All this gave this enterprise a corporate spirit in which the world art workers were united under the leadership of the six cultural executives.

To criticise the sloppy presentation of art works (neighbouring each other by accident) is beside the point. The majority of exhibitions of contemporary Russian art organised around the Biennale were just as badly installed. Regardless of the curators' claim that such international biennales are 'about the role of the curator and their skills in arranging or presenting the information and the works', by now we all know that in the busy industry of making contemporary blockbusters, the designers or in the worst case scenarios (such as the Moscow one) 'production managers', do the job.

One problem was, I believe, that European curators were invited by the ex-Soviet establishment[4] to work on an unknown territory which they desperately and arrogantly—if not ignorantly—tried to define by means of broken epithets cited above. (One wonders how the Russian curators felt about these naïve questions about Russian identity.) For those intent on selling a western product to Russia, attempting to define Russia saved them the task of telling new consumers the story of the troubled western art industry.

The Biennale was rather more successful in its presentation of established artists. The latter were advertised as 'special guests', and they came from three geographic areas: Christian Boltanski from Europe, Bill Viola from the USA, and Ilya Kabakov from Russia (although he now resides in the USA).

Instead of importing one of his often seen installations, Boltanski demonstrated his formal and conceptual methodology to the Russian viewer by conceiving 'Odessa Ghosts'. A sort of deferred visualisation of ancestral horror stories he heard in his childhood, it consisted of black coats hung in the ruined wing of A.V. Shchusev State Museum of Architecture (the same Shchusev who built the Lenin Mausoleum) each dimly lit with naked light bulbs. This pairing of Boltanski's wearisome paraphernalia with the decayed 'Soviet style', transformed both. The vaulted, red brick interior—whose two levels are separated only by rough beams and shabbily laid planks—acquired a captivating atmosphere of a Romanesque space, and the forest of coats from the Salvation Army hinted at the Comme des Garçons merchandise.

The State Museum of Fine Arts, situated across the street from the rebuilt Cathedral of Christ the Saviour, was the similarly appropriate location for Viola's video installation 'The Greeting'. Inspired by a religious painting by the Italian mannerist Jacopo Pontormo, Viola's high-tech 'copy' of a classical painting was in a perfect tune with the original ambition of this museum. Built in 1812, it offered to local art students many copies of Western sculpture. The advanced technology with which Viola's video translated a canonic religious subject matter into a casual contemporary incident, positioned this piece as an effective metaphor for the Russians' refurbished religiousness. Moreover, next to the kitschy reproductions of the icons and frescoes seen in abundance in the nearby cathedral, 'The Greeting' came across as a springboard for anyone who wants to give a thought to how one could reconnect tastefully with a large bulk of the lost religious imagery.

Finally, Kabakov sent to the Biennale organisers a replica of his first installations '16 Ropes' to be reinstalled in his legendary studio on Sretinskii Boulevard. Acting within the framework of the Nietzschean notion of the retreat and return of the origins, Kabakov faced the least expected obstacle. Inaccessible to the general public in 1983, a public viewing of '16 Ropes' was once again spoiled by complicated rules of visitation. This time, though, one could not blame KGB agents who in the Soviet period scared off many potential visitors to the studios of unofficial artists. Such long forgotten state ideological control has now *returned*—this time under the slogan of private property protection, ruling that the gate to the courtyard with the entrance to the staircase leading to Kabakov's studio must be kept locked.

Will alternative Soviet art ever lose its alternative status?

The decision of the Russian curator Joseph Backstein to install '16 Ropes' in Kabakov's studio, and thus keep it outside of local museums, was in line with the position that unofficial artists of Kabakov's generation are presently granted in Russia. Although it has been almost two decades since unofficial art—the notion of which emerged in the late 1950s—began to be shown officially, this institution-less cultural experiment is still not assigned a legitimate institutional niche. In fact, the desire of several curators (notably Sasha Obukhova and Oksana Sarkisyan) and of some new institutions (National Centre for Contemporary Arts and the Drugoe Iskusstvo Museum) to recreate the apartment exhibitions from the Soviet era (as part of the Biennale program), seemed to underline this situation.

There was a brief attempt in the 1990s to collect, interpret, and integrate unofficial art into official museums such as the State Tretiakov Gallery or privately funded Moscow Museum of Contemporary Art. The MMCA is a far from transparent institution. No-one knows what its policy is, except for the creation of an expanded identity-field for the work of its main sponsor and director—Zurab Tseretelli. Regardless of his unspeakably bad taste and lack of talent, Tseretelli has been able to stay on the surface of art talk (in Russia and abroad) for at least a decade. He understood that in order to promote himself on a big scale, he needed to promote many others on a small one. So, during the Biennale, Tseretelli exhibited everything and everyone: live performances and displays of photos with personage scenarios by Monroe (Vladyslav Mamyshev)—the famous infant terrible of *perestroika*, exhibitions exploring gender issues, videos with a feminist agenda, photographs with a homosexual agenda, and émigré artists. All united under the sweep of Tseretelli's 'nouveaux riches' generosity.

The exhibition that the State Tretiakov Gallery offered as a part of the Biennale program, was called *Accomplices. Collective and Interactive Works in Russian Art of the 1960s–2000s*. Organized by the curator-wonderer Andrei Erofeev, it has heavily drawn on the collection of contemporary art (consisting primarily of artists' gifts or extended loans) that he has been single-handedly managing on behalf of various museums. The exhibition's conspiratorial title, its conceptual linearity as well as its sloppy presentation, made it come across as an overview of a fraternal imago of resistance whose members opposed first the repressive cultural rules of the state, and then the involvement of religious orthodoxy in cultural affairs. Unfortunately, the promotion of aesthetics under the aegis of tactile relationships and a shared agenda is always accompanied by a huge amount of rubbish and kitsch. Thus, the 'stars' of unofficial post-war art were dragged into a project that confirmed their perpetual status as institutional outcasts.[5]

From bird's to worm's eye view

Facing the situation where the local institutional establishment as well as academia, are unable to mark discursive zones in pre- and post-Soviet contemporary art, some Moscow artists have taken this project into their own hands. The line of similar attempts undertaken earlier by Russian artists includes a successful re-contextualisation of certain movements in the Russian avant-garde as well as deconstructive reading of ideological myths in official Soviet culture. This time the discourse of abstraction—the high point of modernism—is scrutinised. The particular function of abstract language which is here being tested against the socio-cultural fabric of the new Russia is the one launched by artists of the avant-garde who after the revolution employed their well developed non-objective lexicon to the propaganda needs of Bolshevism.

The two artists who most effectively embark on this experiment (both in theory and practice), are Avdei Ter-Oganyan and Anatolii Osmolovskii. A few years ago Ter-Oganyan was prosecuted by the religious establishment for cutting up paper icons (he avoided the charges by running away to the Czech republic). Not being able to return home, Ter-Oganyan joined the list—from Herzen to Lenin—of exiled Russian radicals whose critique of societal ills becomes only more effective from a distance. He exhibited a series of photographs in 'Russia 2' (an ambitious exhibition of local artists that positioned itself in competition with the Biennale) under the title 'Radical Abstractions'. Here he exchanged concrete religious and political iconography for supposedly neutral geometric forms and assigned to these abstract compositions a written statement that activated each of them as a weapon against the political or religious establishment. This way Ter-Oganyan reminded Russian viewers that although abstraction may seem today to be decorative and neutralised and a desirable aesthetic expression, it was only recently perceived by most of them as the realm of cultural decadence and danger. So if Ter-Oganyan's cutting up paper icons stirred up the issue of how the zealous Soviet atheism quickly transformed itself into just as zealous religiousness, 'Radical Abstractions' put the brakes on the speeding machine that successfully erases the traces of a variety of former cultural and political ruptures.

The new abstract works of Osmolovskii are in line with the same argument as he insists that 'abstract art...is an expanded demonstration of an absence of an individual freedom'.[6] However, unlike Ter-Oganyan, Osmolovsky adopted the kind of abstract forms—offered with titles such as 'Pieces', or 'Nails'—that fall into the framework of George Bataille's notion of 'formless', or Melanie Klein's concept of 'part-objects'. If by climbing in 1994 the extra tall statue of the poet Vladimir Mayakovskii, Osmolovsky aspired to seizing the bird's eye view upon the twentieth-century cultural heritage—Russian and western alike—then with his new series of formless objects Osmolovskii descends to the position of the worm's eye view. From this more humble vantage point he localises Bataille's conclusion that 'affirming that the universe resembles nothing and is only *formless* amounts to saying that the universe is something like a spider or spit…for academic men to be happy, the universe would have to take shape'.[7]

Russia 2

Perhaps the six Biennale curators will in two years' time (for it's already been decided that they will all return to do the second Biennale) answer their own loaded question 'who are the Russians?'. But given that the notion of Russianness fluctuated for centuries, I would, first, re-phrase the question by asking 'who are the Russians *now*?'. Russians are the people who were able to surprise everyone by launching *Perestroika*, and yet were unable to complete it. Russians are persuasive enough to make western feminists be softer on men, and Jacques Derrida confess his secret love for logocentrism.[8] Russians have, in less than two decades, translated and published numerous books on post-war western philosophy which among other things taught us to recognise the power of context in processing mimetic representations; yet, when it comes to exhibiting Robert Mapplethorpe (also as part of the Biennale program), they choose to conceal well-known controversy over his images in the neutralising atmosphere of the Hermitage masterworks. Some Russians have such a widespread reputation for being money spenders that the hottest designers flock to Moscow with merchandise that is unavailable in many European capitals; other Russians are tolerant enough to have their neighbourhood groceries be replaced by design stores where most of them cannot afford shopping. Russians are dragged into the local culture industry before they are provided with an educational system and a museum capable of facilitating their understanding of Modern Art. And finally, yet, not exhaustively, Russians are undoubtedly uncanny in their commitment to maintain Lenin's dead body in the mausoleum, and are probably sufficiently outlandish to launch a competition for a design of the leader's new suit.

Notes

1. 'Introduction' in *Dialectics of Hope: 1 Moscow Biennale of Contemporary Art* (Moscow: ArtChronika, 2005), no pagination. Subsequent citations are also from this Introduction.
2. In 1924 Shchusev designed two versions of wooden mausoleums, one of which was built in 1924. It was replaced by a marble structure in 1930.
3. 'Introduction', *Dialectics of Hope*.

4. It is important to remember that the Biennale was organised and supported by the Ministry of Culture and other official cultural and political institutions in order to establish Russia as an equal player on the arena of international art business, including the now common industry of turning up surveys of global contemporary art practices.

5. For a further discussion of both museums, see Margarita Tupitsyn, 'Moscow: On the Ruins of the Third Museum' in *Third Text*, vol.17, no.4 (2003), pp.379–88.

6. Anatoly Osmolovsky, *Iskusstvo bez opravdanii* (Moscow, 2004), p.16.

7. Georges Bataille (ed. and trans Allan Stoekl), *Visions of Excess: Selected Writings, 1927–1939* (Minneapolis, 1985), p.31.

8. See Victor Tupitsyn, 'Derrida in Moscow', *Parallax*, 3 (September 1996), pp.146–9.

Reviews

Gwynne Lewis, *France 1715–1804. Power and the People* (Longman, London & New York, 2004), ISBN 0–582–23925–7, 307pp., £19.99 pbk.

Gwynne Lewis's latest work has been written with one eye on a student readership and provides an admirably lucid and comprehensive coverage of the social, economic and intellectual developments in eighteenth-century France. Yet this is far more than an introductory text book. Students, specialists and general readers will all be stimulated and informed by his powerful rebuttal of revisionist and postmodern attempts to detach the revolution from the profound blockages and tensions which beset the *ancien régime*. Despite a genuflection in the direction of those who emphasise the climatic instability of the pre-revolutionary years and other contingent causes, Lewis's analysis hinges on the failure to resolve long-term structural and social problems.

Not that he merely resurrects social interpretations of the revolution associated with such classic expositors as Georges Lefebvre or Albert Soboul. His study is impressively up-to-date, resting for a large part on a substantial amount of historical writing accomplished over the last decade. This is fashioned into a finely tuned synthesis, sustaining some older views whilst giving weight to material which requires their modification. In no doubt that the demise of the *ancien régime* cannot be understood without reference to the pressures generated by capitalism, both within and without France, his picture of its progress steers an imaginative course through a complex topic. Industrial capitalism may have been developing slowly in France but it was developing. Furthermore, the effects of proto-industrialisation have been widely underestimated whilst 'the depiction of the French economy as composed of a booming periphery and a stagnant centre requires major revision' (p.95). If it is true that France entered the consumerist society 'on the backs of the court and the aristocracy' (p.106) this nonetheless meant that in the 'production of luxury goods, porcelain wines and brandies she was one of the most advanced countries in the world' (p.98).

The emergence of capitalism also contributed together with significant cultural and political changes, partly encapsulated in Habermas's notion of the public sphere, to the partial formation of a bourgeois consciousness amongst a heterogeneous group encompassing the liberal professions, financiers, merchants and artisans. However 'the permeability of class barriers in France, as well as the way in which power was distributed through the court, the Church and the professional corporations, masked the gradual formation of a cohesive bourgeois identity' (p.114) which would only materialise in the revolutionary confrontation with aristocratic elites. Recognising the value of the now widely held view that the revolution made the bourgeoisie rather than the other way round, Lewis faces up to the consequent need to explain from whence came this bourgeoisie.

The emergence of capitalism contributed to the difficulties of a state which, whilst displaying features of an emergent 'proto-modern' (p.24) bureaucracy, was constrained by the crown's willingness, in return for the support of the nobility, to sustain the landed system on which they depended. Amongst the most striking pages in the book are those dealing with the counter-productive consequences of the precocious and immature injection of capitalism into an unreceptive milieu by John Law during the regency government (1715–23). Yet as late as the 1760s the Duc de Choiseul struggled to introduce a reform movement designed to rescue France from the humiliating defeat of the Seven Years War and which sought to emulate England's movement towards 'free trade and aristocratic, constitutional government' (p.171). Although physiocratic arguments in favour of economic liberalisation had overcome the mercantilist attachment to regulation, Turgot also failed, a decade later, to implement his reform programme. Despite determined efforts, on which Lewis casts some fascinating light, the marriage of liberal capitalism with Bourbon monarchism was beyond reach.

On the other hand, to the extent that the grain trade was freed and protectionist policies were abandoned in the pre-revolutionary years, the effect was to exacerbate the rising tide of poverty (barely mentioned in some recent treatments of the *ancien régime*) which threatened, at times, to overwhelm more than a half of the population. Whilst recognising that neither peasantry nor urban workers were uniformly or always poverty stricken Lewis is insistent that 'the failure to respond to the plight of the poor and the dispossessed proved to be the single most destabilising socio-political problem confronting the Bourbon monarchy' (p.116). A detailed analysis of those who made up the 'fourth estate' of poverty is followed by discussion of the rising tempo and scale of popular protest during the 1760s and 1770s, a significant prelude to the explosion of 1789. The government responded on the one hand with ferociously repressive measures and on the other by retreating from its programme of economic liberalisation.

The revolutionaries did not fare much better in confronting the problems of poverty and agrarian reform. The alliance of Jacobins and people proved short lived. The subsequent exclusion of 'le peuple' from power meant that the first revolution to be accomplished, according to Lewis, in part by popular intervention from below, ended in defeat for the 'Rights of the Common Man'. By 1799 'the choice for many poor young men was either to be killed by the army or to join it' (p.260). Neither the revolution nor free-market capitalism achieved a real democracy and even a welfare state remained a distant prospect.

Readers weary of attempts to deconstruct the French revolution will be immensely grateful to Lewis. His powers of persuasion are remarkable, all the better for touches of wit. Apart from odd details, for instance about the length of peasant leases, and occasionally provocative judgments, the only significant passage in which his case is not convincingly made is perhaps in the association of poverty with the religious passions of the 1730s.

Yet readers of marxist persuasion or those wishing to know exactly how Lewis would categorise his own methodology may be perplexed by his occasional theoretical observations. Despite a passing, perhaps ironical, reference to 'historians who seek to rescue French history from the enfeebled hands of Marxist interpretations of history' (p.32), his own view of the way in which capitalism developed within traditional structures that were increasingly unable to accommodate it might be derived directly from Marx and Engels. More puzzling, is the expressed preference for an approach which stresses the interaction of the political, social and intellectual as opposed to one which stresses conflict between classes (p. 2). They are surely not incompatible. Lewis understandably distances himself from structuralist definitions of class which takes them as given. Yet his analysis not only contains helpful observations about class formation but conveys with conviction the exploitation and domination of the producers by the privileged. It is difficult to see precisely why it 'is more illuminating to analyse eighteenth century France in terms of Orders and estates and rather than classes related to changing modes of production'. Indeed, the placing of inverted commas around his pivotal 'fourth estate of poverty' suggests a major difficulty for such a view. Nor is this resolved by some shifting formulations about the traditional socio-economic system which Lewis describes variously as a 'post feudal system of land exploitation' (p.64), ' an anachronistic feudal land system' (p.66), an imploding feudal system' (p.100) and 'a decaying, pre-capitalist landed system' (p.17). Given the trenchant observation that it took the revolutionaries four years (1789–93), a European war and several major peasant uprisings to dispense with feudal property rights, the qualifying adjectives might have been ditched. They are, in any case, insignificant in the context of a superbly sustained and very timely elaboration of the powerful forces which both made and constrained the revolution.

David Parker
University of Leeds

David Renton, *Sidney Pollard. A Life in History* (London, Tauris Academic Studies, 2004), ISBN 1–85043–453–0, ix+210pp., £45, hbk.

Sidney Pollard was a prolific historian. The valuable bibliography in David Renton's biography runs to nearly 200 items without ephemera and unpublished materials. But was Pollard worth a biography? He was an economic historian who wrote extensively on British economic history after 1750; the development of the labour relations and patterns of European industrialisation. He also tried to carry his arguments into the wider arena with sustained attacks on the de-industrialisation of Britain and what he saw as the malign influence of the City and the 'banker's mentality'. But few in Britain would have thought of him as being in the first rank of historians of his time. This is partly because, although he addressed big themes, his strength appeared to lay in a concern with details. There is no 'Pollard approach' save perhaps his work on European industrialisation and even here the strengths arise from the detail rather than the overall coherence. But the reception of Pollard's work in Britain perhaps reflects something else. Renton quotes Eric Hobsbawm puzzling over Pollard's 'shameful neglect', 'I cannot entirely understand the reason. In my view he was certainly one of the most distinguished and original economic historians we have had in my lifetime'. Renton does not entirely explain this either. Perhaps Pollard just didn't work hard enough or in the right ways to carry his arguments more forcefully? But perhaps a fuller explanation would also have to address the continuing way in which the visible part of British intellectual life still depends on a narrow circle focused on London, Oxford and Cambridge. Pollard, a child refugee from fascism in 1938, had some of the characteristics to make his mark here; his mistake (less obvious to those outside the UK) could have been to spend so much of his life in 'provincial Sheffield'.

But even if Pollard had only been a talented and hard working historian his career would have been of some interest and Renton's account takes us effortlessly through the development of British economic history in the fifty years after 1945. The book was only possible because Pollard's papers were deposited at the University of Sunderland by his widow. Too often libraries in new universities have renamed themselves learning centres and refused or disposed of stock to make way for those computers which now look increasingly redundant as more students buy their own. Sunderland too may have gone down this road but they appear not to have forgotten the importance of preservation and they deserve praise for this.

Not the least intriguing aspect of Renton's account is the way in which it puts a personal side to some of the big names of British economic history. Pollard was in part a victim of the pettiness of occasionally lesser historians who disliked his politics whose left character they seemed to imagine was greater than it was. Few will fail to be moved by the account of the way in which a brief student flirtation with the British Communist Party as well as friendship with the GDR historian Jurgen Kuczynski, led to his moment of triumph being snatched away from him. This was the offer of a chair at Berkeley in 1971. When he then faced US visa difficulties—perhaps not that great in comparative terms—they created an emotional storm, bringing back his 'orphaning' flight from Austria and the loss of his parents in the concentration camps.

> My encounter has brought up, out of the forgotten traumas of the past, such horrors of queuing in offices, of being a second-class citizen, of fearing the decisions of capricious officialdom, as I never thought I still had in me, and I suffered an almost total collapse over it.

But he recovered his momentum to spend more years at Sheffield and to reap more international recognition with ten years in Germany at Bielefeld before retiring back to the area that had become his home.

Renton describes Pollard as 'a socialist of sorts'. But Pollard was also a theorist of sorts so that an evaluation of his contribution requires us to have a wider sense of how his work fits in. Since neither Pollard, nor Renton, nor this reviewer has a confident 'big theory' this is difficult. Renton finds it easiest to deal with Pollard's contribution to the history of labour and management because here there is rough agreement on what the story is. Renton is less positive about Pollard's critique of the role of policy in British relative economic decline suggesting that 'life itself' has undermined Pollard's argument for maintaining a strong manufacturing base. But it may not be this simple. Britain is still in the premier league of manufacturing powers. Moreover if its base has been slimmed further in relative terms than other advanced economies there may be an element of luck here rather than a model. In the same way that the Hong-Kong/Singapore model is of limited relevance to most economies, Europe too possibly only has room for one offshore financial-service economy. More challenging still, if problematic, is Pollard's regional approach to industrialisation. This is possibly his least known contribution in the UK—a reflection of our parochialism—but it was the centre of his attention in his later years. Pollard saw industrialisation as a process of regional change within the developing global economy with nation states playing ambiguous intermediary roles. The difficulty, which he could not solve, was to clearly articulate the relationship of these three elements—region, state and global economy—but his sense of the importance of this problem remains to be built upon.

Faced with the modern avalanche of publications to which we all contribute I have found myself going back to older generations of historians. I have been continually surprised at how good they were. Arguments may sometimes be disagreeable, even plain wrong, the style and technique may be different but the real content is no worse and often better than what we all produce today. I suspect that in fifty years' times those who find Pollard's books and articles on dusty shelves will still feel the effort worthwhile and if they have been guided to them by coming across Renton's biography of him on another equally dusty shelf, then potted and careless in writing and referencing though it occasionally is, it too will have served a longer-term purpose.

Mike Haynes
University of Wolverhampton

Dave Harker, *Tressell: The Real Story of the Ragged Trousered Philanthropists* (Zed Books, London, 2003), ISBN 1–84277–385–2, 282+xx pp., £12.99 pbk, £50 hbk.

What did the Communist Party ever do for *The Ragged Trousered Philanthropists* (apart from rescuing, publishing, promoting, dramatising, popularising, criticising and televising it)?

Tressell: The Real Story of the Ragged Trousered Philanthropists has many virtues. Harker successfully roots Tressell's novel in the grim world of the pre–1914 British left, its sectarian divisions and fantasy politics. His account of the book's publishing history is thorough and compelling. And there are some delightful details—*The Ragged Trousered Philanthropists* selling eight times more copies than James Joyce's *Dubliners* (also published by Grant Richards in 1914). Tom Thomas negotiating with the Lord Chamberlain's office for a maximum of sixteen 'bloodys' in his stage version of the novel, the CP building worker in Liverpool who, though 'often the worse for drink', sold over 500 copies of the novel.

Best of all are the testimonies of dozens of readers, some famous but mostly anonymous, on the role of the novel in their political education. Although these are not sourced, these letters are presumably the results of Kathleen Noonan's 1977 appeal for readers of her father's novel to write to her. Harker's use of his access to the Tressell family papers is this book's real strength.

However, Harker's second source is more problematic. It consists of one letter and two tape-cassettes recorded by the poet Jack Beeching shortly before his death in 2001. Originally from Hastings, Beeching's grandfather had worked with men who had known Tressell. He was once a member of the Communist Party and, as a director of Lawrence & Wishart, was party to some of the discussions about the publication of the unabridged novel. But Jack Beeching was a better poet than a memoirist. His published memoir of the US poet Tom McGrath is notoriously unreliable. In old age his memories were characterised by anti-communism and personal animus.

Not that any of this is a problem for Harker, who is less interested in *The Ragged Trousered Philanthropists* as a work of fiction than he is in the book's politics, or more specifically the political uses to which it has been put (he accuses Jack Jones, for example, of using the novel as 'left cover' for his attachment to the Labour Party). Above all, *Tressell: The Real Story* is a sustained caricature of the 'philistine' Communist Party and the bad faith of its cultural organisations. In fact, Harker has hardly anything to say about the novel as a novel—its mix of voices, forms and traditions, styles and narrative tricks, its borrowings and its imitators or its sheer *oddness*. It might have been worth comparing it to fiction by other Edwardian socialists like Patrick MacGill and Jack London, or by the next generation of working-class novelists like Jack Hilton (who also wrote about the building trade) or Walter Greenwood (whose Larry Meath was clearly descended from Tressell's Owen). None of the working-class novelists published by Lawrence & Wishart in 1955 at the same time as their unexpurgated edition of *The Ragged Trousered Philanthropists* appear in the index. On the other hand, Stalin appears fifteen times.

As a result, the book switches abruptly and sometimes comically between the history of the novel and bits of unrelated, superficial and selective historical 'background'. From the General Strike to New Labour, British history only ever demonstrates the 'treachery' of trade union leaders and the 'abject' nature of the CP. Tressell's socialism, of course, turns out to have nothing in common with either the Labour Party or 'Russian communism'.

Not only has *The Ragged Trousered Philanthropists* 'survived the crisis of Stalinism', but Tony Cliff liked it! (It was, apparently, a good example of 'propaganda aimed at the workers rather than the left intellectual milieu'.) There is something touchingly Spartish about all this—the *Manchester Guardian* is 'the capitalist press', Arthur Scargill is a 'Stalinist', Eileen Yeo is the voice of 'pessimistic bourgeois feminism'. This provides occasional moments of Tressell-like slap-stick bathos, as when Harker's discussion of Tom Thomas's adaptation of the novel for the stage is immediately followed by a stern and stirring section on 'The Final and Absolute Submission to Stalin'.

The book claims that the 'post-war history of *RTP* is bound up with that of the Communist Party'. But it never explains what this means. Crucially missing is an account of the complex and contradictory ways in which Zhdanovism impacted on CP intellectual and cultural life in the Cold War. The 'Battle of Ideas' may have been imposed from Moscow, but the CP needed no encouragement to explore national democratic cultural traditions or a novel like *The Ragged Trousered Philanthropists*. Such concerns had been at the heart of the party's cultural arguments at least since the mid-1930s. Moreover, it coincided with a growing feeling among communist writers that it was time to put some critical distance between the British party and the Cominform. But Harker, of course, cannot accept the idea that CP writers were ever anything other than slaves to Stalin. He authoritatively refutes the idea of a 'cultural opposition' inside the party during the 1950s by pointing out that fifteen years earlier the editors of *Left Review* had once refused to accept an advert for a book about Trotsky.

Just once Harker hints that Jack Beeching may have promoted *The Ragged Trousered Philanthropists* as a coded way of criticising 'Popular Frontism' (and by extension the *British Road to Socialism*) inside the CP. But this is never developed. In fact Harker goes to such lengths to demonstrate the complete, irremediable and inexcusable uselessness of the CP that it is hard to imagine how it could have been responsible for anything at all. He is especially hard on Lawrence & Wishart, who published the first unexpurgated edition of the novel in 1955 (subsequently reprinted sixteen times), both of Fred Ball's biographies of Tressell as well as Jack Mitchell's first book-length study of the novel. Harker's complaint seems to be that L&W hesitated for several years before publishing the full novel because of the legal and financial risks involved. But what publisher doesn't think like this—in the early 1970s L&W apparently considered publishing a shortened version of the novel for use in schools, but were deterred by printing costs. Harker's take on this is that 'At the height of a period of industrial struggle comparable only to 1926, it was a risk Lawrence and Wishart were not prepared to take. They closed the project down.' 'How,' Harker asks significantly, 'do we explain Lawrence and Wishart's...pessimism ?' Unfortunately he never answers the question (apart from quoting Beeching to the effect that no-one at the firm had 'any brains').

Perhaps he doesn't need to. In his cartoon history, the CP only ever deserves contempt and ridicule and every communist is a 'Stalinist' and 'a shit', whose every act is open to sinister interpretation. For example, he notes darkly that *The Ragged Trousered Philanthropists* was not on the reading-list of a CP training manual in 1927; that in 1933 '*RTP* fan Wal Hannington was forced off the CPGB's Central Committee'; that Tommy Jackson did not even *mention* the novel in *Old Friends to Keep*. According to Harker, Lawrence & Wishart had a devious 'policy of publishing tactfully edited novels under working-class writers' names' (who *does* he mean?) While Lawrence & Wishart were still debating whether to publish the unabridged version in 1952, 'elements of the CP hierarchy' 'joined in' (this turns out to mean that Walter Holmes supported the idea in the *Daily Worker*).

The more the 'Stalinists' did to popularise the novel, the less credit Harker is prepared to give them. He tells us that 'the Stalinist authorities did not like its "critical spirit"', and yet *The Ragged Trousered Philanthropists* was published in the Soviet Union, the GDR, Czechoslovakia (where it was also televised) and Bulgaria. Jack Mitchell completed his PhD thesis on the book at Humboldt University in the GDR. A pirate edition of the novel was published in the Soviet Union as early as the 1920s.

But Harker reserves his greatest condemnation for those whom he is pleased to call 'CP "intellectuals"'. He tell us that 'British Communist intellectuals remained timid about the book' (but in the next two sentences he quotes Jack Lindsay and Arnold Kettle on the novel's importance). Prevented by their Stalinism from recognising the novel's message of hope, they variously criticised its lack of subtlety, saw it as part of a distinctively English literary tradition, described it as 'tragic realism' and 'socialist realism', and generally did everything they could to water it down. For decades, almost the only literary critics to write about the novel at any length were communists—Fred Ball, Tommy Jackson, Jack Mitchell, David Craig, Mary Ashraf, Len Jones and Jeremy Hawthorn. Stuart Douglas (who wrote the 1967 television adaptation for BBC2) worked for *Labour Monthly*. But their contribution to Tressell's memory and to the reputation of the novel pales into insignificance when you think that the SWP once had a bookstall at a Robert Tressell event in Hastings.

Andy Croft

Andy Croft's recent book of poems is Comrade Laughter *(Flambard Press)*

Norman LaPorte, *The German Communist Party in Saxony, 1924–1933. Factionalism, Fratricide and Political Failure* (Peter Lang, Bern, 2003), ISBN 3–906768–45–7, 399pp., £37 pbk.

Saxony in the south of central Germany, according to pre-Second World War frontiers, was one of the earliest industrialised parts of Germany. Together with neighbouring Thuringia it constituted the main region of origin of the social-democratic movement some century and a half ago. Consequently, the new communist movement resulting from the split within social democracy during the First World War had an important stronghold there. In both states in the early 1920s, the SPD and KPD succeeded between them in winning a parliamentary majority which during the crucial year of 1923 was supposed to be the starting point of a victorious German 'October revolution'. This failed abysmally as was recently documented in a volume presenting original material from the Comintern archive, which unfortunately appeared only after the volume under review had been published. The once dominant workers' movement in Saxony suffered a deep crisis at this time and lost its majority support in the population while experiencing serious confrontations between its revolutionary and reformist wings. At the same time, the KPD itself went through a series of faction fights. When in 1929 the world economic crisis began, the once red Saxony very rapidly took on the brown colour of the National Socialists.

Norman LaPorte, who teaches at the University of Glamorgan, has presented a meticulously researched study of the Communist Party's development in this crucial Land, from the aftermath of 'German October's' disaster to the establishment of the Nazi dictatorship. While basing his research principally on the party records which became available after the end of the GDR and are now deposited in the Federal Archives, he also makes good use of the vast amount of research published so far mainly (though not exclusively) in Germany. This does not only concern the history of Saxony, and notably its economic and political development since the nineteenth century. Most of all it concerns the huge KPD historiography of the last decades, not only at the Reich level, but even more so at the regional and local level in other parts of the Germany. LaPorte makes use of this literature to present alternative interpretations within which to situate his own research.

To summarise very briefly, two theories have more or less successively dominated the historiography, as LaPorte outlines in some detail in his introduction. On the one hand, there was the 'stalinisation' paradigm which saw the party as a top-down enterprise shaped by decisions made in Moscow and which emphasised the epidemic leadership struggles and the confrontation with social democracy. The other approach, 'from below', concentrated on the place of the party in the wider working-class life, stressed local and regional factors and looked for evidence of proletarian community beyond political cleavages. According to this interpretation, political strategies would grow out of this context rather than being imposed from outside. In providing a comprehensive overview of the existing literature, which should be especially useful for readers without knowledge of German, LaPorte concentrates almost exclusively for the pre-1989 period on historiographical debates in West Germany. That he makes such scant use of the GDR literature, essentially comprising local studies, confirms that it was largely incapable of offering an understanding of the party's fate.

Of course, many considerations flow into these two divergent models of interpretation. One was the shift from political history 'from above' to social and, later, cultural history. Different generational experiences, notably manifested in the influence of different political attitudes), were exacerbated by generational competition for the ever-decreasing amount of jobs in history departments. Admittedly, of all this makes it difficult sometimes to attribute complex research projects to one of these fixed models. On the other hand, these two historiographical theories of how to understand the KPD will certainly remind those working on other parties or on the international movement in general of similar controversies in their own field.

LaPorte, however, thinks rightly that it is time to progress to a new synthesis, to what he calls a post-revisionist approach, to fuse history 'from above and below'. On the one hand, he makes it clear that the Comintern agenda was set in Moscow and that its general strategy was developed according to needs there which had little or nothing to do with the concrete expectations of the rank and file of the party under consideration. Nevertheless, he also regards it as an important task to examine whether there were interrelations between 'top' and 'bottom' and whether, and if so how, a party leadership tried to find a room to manoeuvre when they realised the possible liabilities of Comintern policy, even if they did not dare to question the whole strategy.

This introduction to LaPorte's methodology and the existing historiography is followed by a short setting of the scene. He explains the political landscape in which the party operated and briefly outlines the socio-economic conditions in this *Land*, which, with its export-orientated and essentially middle-sized industry, was especially disfavoured by the post-war economy. The bulk of the narrative then comprises a meticulous reconstruction of the party's travail. The recurrent themes are indicated in the

subtitle of the book: *Factionalism* meant that the party succumbed to a continuous internal struggle between the 'left', mainly antagonistic to a united front
with the SPD, and a 'right', fighting for it. At least in the first years after 1924,
this situation was aggravated by the fact that each faction controlled a sector
of the party apparatus in Saxony, namely one of the districts into which the
party was divided. The existing factions, on the other hand, reflected the different political and socioeconomic milieux in which the party was operating.
That is, if the party had obtained a position of strength, it could force the SPD
into certain united front activities. Usually this meant the existence of a common ground, a wider workers' movement, in which the communists held
strong positions. This sector of the party tended to the right. However, where
the party was weak and the SPD could neglect the communists (a tendency
to which the strong Austromarxist leaning in parts of Saxony's SPD also contributed), the KPD tended to the left and employed the united front as a simple
denunciation of 'bankrupt reformism'. As the instructions coming from
Berlin, and beyond that Moscow, demanded a uniform appearance of the
party, favouring in 1924–5 very 'left' tactics, which then were somewhat moderated, this led to a continuous faction fight—or did so at least until the party
was made completely subservient around 1928–9.

Fratricide refers to the results of all this in the party's zigzags towards the
SPD and its sphere of influence in the wider workers' movement. Given the
above mentioned differences in pursuing sincere united front politics, it was
impossible for the KPD to exploit the SPD's crisis in 1926, when its right wing
split to enter a coalition with the bourgeois parties in the Saxon parliament.
Similarly the KPD failed with its different unity offers during the campaign
that same year to expropriate the former Princely Houses or, at the trade union
level, during the strike wave of 1928 which foreshadowed the outbreak of the
economic crisis in the following year. Unfortunately, though, the trade union
field is not as systematically covered as it deserves to be in constituting the
main 'outreach work' of the communists. In this respect, LaPorte concentrates
too exclusively on the 'highlights' in the economic struggle.

With *political failure* he sums up the 'third period' after 1928, the policies of
'social fascism' and separate 'red trade unions' and the inability to grasp prop-
erly the significance of the Nazi onslaught. Different tactical variations were
developed, like the use of nationalism to appeal to the radicalised middle
classes which had constantly moved to the right after the workers' movement's
self-inflicted defeat in 1923. Whereas at the street level the party was engaged
in violent clashes with the storm troopers, its propaganda theorised about
'social fascism as the main enemy' on the road to the revolution. Setbacks
for the party could then be explained only by sabotage or ideological inade-

quacies in the apparatus due to secret adherents of whatever the deviation might be. Appropriately, LaPorte gives the title '*Götterdämerung*' (twilight of the gods) to this last section.

Consequently in his conclusion he makes it clear that his 'post-revisionist' approach is not about the party line being derived from endogenous conditions such as reflecting the desperate situation of the unemployed etc. Repeatedly and convincingly he makes it clear that the turn of 1928-9 in particular, though resembling some earlier cases, was imposed on the party from outside. Nevertheless, the usefulness of his accounts lies in his reconstruction of the ways in which the changes were implemented, the variations in the response from the party rank and file—anything but a homogenous group— and the consequences this had for the relationship of forces in the workers' movement in general.

Unfortunately, though this work contains many insights crying out for a comparative analysis, this dimension is provided only incidentally, limited to the development of the KPD in other regions or at the Reich level and the different interpretations to which it has given arise. With regard to communism beyond Germany, however, this dimension is absent from his account. Given the huge amount of research on which it is already based, this is perhaps too demanding. Nevertheless, hopefully the considerations offered in this book will provide a contribution to such reflections in the future.

All in all, this is an important study of a key segment of Germany's communist movement during a crucial period. With its rich and detailed accumulation of facts and names it is essentially a specialist book. Possibly the reader looking for a more general understanding of the movement's fate during this period might easily get lost in the amount of the detail provided, especially as the book unfortunately lacks a name index. On the other hand, such a reader will be helped by the fact that the narrative is mainly developed on chronological lines.

Reiner Tosstorff

William J. Fishman, *East End Jewish Radicals 1875–1914* (Five Leaves, Nottingham, 2004), ISBN 0–90712–345–7, 340pp., £14.99 pbk; **Rudolf Rocker**, *The London Years* (Five Leaves, Nottingham, 2004), ISBN 0–90712–330–9, 304pp., £14.99 pbk.

The reprints of Bill Fishman's *East End Jewish Radicals* and Rudolf Rocker's *The London Years* are a timely reminder that prejudice against aliens and foreigners continues down the ages. Both books provide deep insights into an extraordinary period of struggle by immigrant workers to win a decent standard of living for their families, and dignity and respect for themselves. Through this struggle they were able to block the worst excesses of the anti-alien campaign of the time.

Rocker's book reminded me of a seventy-year old tailor I worked with in the mid-1930s. His view was that Rocker had the best mind, but his favourite was Kaplan, the orator and union leader who figures prominently in the latter part of Fishman's account. Both of them were anarchists.

East European Jews had been known in the East End since the 1860s, when they began to settle in Whitechapel and Spitalfields. The area between them and the city was settled by Dutch Jews, a tightly knit group. The eastern wards of the city had been settled by Spanish and Portuguese Jews two hundred years earlier. They were the workers of Anglo-Jewry. My grandfather said that it was a long time before he could talk to the new immigrants as they spoke Yiddish, which he had never heard. The leadership of Anglo-Jewry—the Rothschilds, Montefiores, Montagues—became involved with the immigrants when their activities began to appear troublesome. The publicity given the sweated trades caused particular embarrassment.

The mass immigration of *East* European Jews began in the 1870s, reaching a high point between 1891 and 1901. The Tsar's pogroms continued and intensified, ensuring a continuous and increasing flow of people to Britain, settling in Leeds, Manchester and Glasgow as well as London. This influx led to appalling housing conditions, particularly in Whitechapel, where many houses also contained workrooms. Though the movement out to the neighbouring areas of Stepney Green, St Georges and Bethnal Green did provide some alleviation of the conditions, rents in the East End increased whether the landlord was Jew or non-Jew, just as prices in the shops followed the same pattern irrespective of ownership.

The response to this immigration, particularly by local Conservative MPs, was to start an anti-alien immigration campaign based on ignorance and fear. Force was used by the thugs of the British Boys. English socialists opposed this campaign and the high point of unity was the demonstration in protest at the Kishinev Pogrom in 1903, when 25,000 East End Jews marched through London supported by leading British socialists. Nevertheless, the Aliens Act was passed into law in 1905—and looking around today it seems as if the leopard does not change its spots.

Among the socialists were an increasing number of socialists committed to improve living and working conditions. These were confronted by a reactionary religious leadership who were opposed to any political or social change which they saw as a threat to their control. The frontal attack on religion frightened many people who saw religion as a safety net and this was sometimes an obstacle to their participation in their struggle to improve conditions.

The first Hebrew socialist union was established by Aaron Leiberman in 1872. Its aim was 'to spread socialism among the Jew and non-Jew'. Despite his commitment to unite all workers against their oppressors, Leiberman was a very difficult man to work with and for personal reasons he went to America, where he died in 1880. However he had influenced and befriended the young Morris Winchevsky who founded the *Poilisce Yidl*, the Yiddish socialist journal, in 1884. Though the journal lasted for only sixteen issues, in 1885 Winchevsky established the *Arbeiter Fraint* which was to become the key organising Yiddish paper. Founded as a paper open to all socialists, in 1886 it passed into the control of the International Workers' Educational Club and became a weekly covering a wide range of subjects. After a bitter sectarian battle, it passed into the control of the anarchists in 1892.

Though some described this as economism, and it was generally held that the more terrible the conditions, the more revolutionary the workers, the socialist organisations believed the first step in the struggle was trade union organisation. The main industry was clothing, where the work operations had been broken down into skilled, semi-skilled and unskilled workers to increase productivity and output. The original production unit had been the family, and though there remained some bespoke tailors, the immigrants' changes to production methods fitted in with the rapidly increasing market for ready-made clothing. The biggest development, however, was in men's wear in Leeds; in London men's wear was dominated by small shops for another twenty years. As for the women's wear industry, this was destabilised by the alternation of two seasons of work and two periods of unemployment. The master tailor received his work from the city wholesalers, who had one concern: making the greatest profit. The new immigrant, the Greener, further weakened the workers' position. The Greener would start work which would continue in the evening when the Guvnor would tell him to work till the candle went out.

Things began to change towards the end of the 1880s. There were strikes in the East End of the women of Bryant & Mays, the gas workers and the dockers. In 1889 the tailors also struck. Though trade union organisation was small and weak, nevertheless there was wide support for the workers' demands of reduced hours, increased pay, limited overtime and union recognition. The dockers contributed £100 to their funds and the exposure of conditions in the sweated trades influenced Rothschild's decision to donate £1,000 and the Jewish establishment to encourage a settlement. Except for union recognition, the demands were agreed—but the failure of this one meant that the other gains were shortlived.

A few years later there arrived in the East End the anarchist Rudolf Rocker, a German Catholic bookbinder who had worked in much of Europe and who in 1898 became editor of the *Arbeiter Fraint*, for which he had to learn Hebrew. The paper's sales increased and within a year a short-lived magazine called *Germinal* appeared, dealing with art, literature and history and demonstrating the stress placed on education of all the socialist groups. The object was to help people think, analyse and evaluate, and to develop an understanding of the progressive achievements of all peoples—a far cry from the current educational orthodoxy of training people as industrial and commercial cannon fodder.

Throughout the period 1900–14 considerable gains were made by the unions, the bakers as well as the tailors, and after the tailors' strike of 1906, though the settlement reached was never applied, the unity established of the two English unions proved a significant achievement which was to pay great dividends. Politically, the most influential organisation was that of the anarchists under Rocker's leadership and Rocker played a key role in the watershed year of 1912. In April of that year, some 1200 highly skilled bespoke tailors in the West End had come out on strike for improved pay and conditions and within a month 8,000 were out. To be successful, however, the strike needed the support of the East End workers mainly working in women's wear, who came out with their own demands after a mass meeting on 8 May. Within the month their demands had been met and the sweating system suffered a grievous blow, though the struggle carried on in the form of the dockers' strike, in which the Jewish socialist organisations were again active in solidarity work. I am sure that Jack London would have been proud if he had been in Whitechapel in 1912 and seen the people march out of the Abyss with heads held high.

The loss of Rocker to America weakened the anarchists and the change in the lives of the immigrants' first and second generation of children also saw changes in the social and political approach. By this time the East End Labour movement had produced its own giants like George Lansbury, whom people could look up to and who helped bring the new generations into the recently formed political organisation of labour. These invaluable reprints serve as a fitting reminder of an earlier period in which a tradition of struggle was established in the most difficult conditions, of chronic poverty, fragile political organisation, and language, ethnic and occupational differences. The unity that was nevertheless achieved by the time of the 1912 strike was to ensure the East End's solidarity against Mosley in 1936.

Ben Birnbaum

Peter Scholliers and Leonard Schwarz, *Experiencing Wages: Social and Cultural Aspects of Wage Forms in Europe since 1500* (Berghahn Books, New York, Oxford, 2003). ISBN 1–57181–546–5, £50.00 hbk, ISBN 1–57181–547–3, £15.00 pbk.

The forms of wages are the expression of social relations in the production process, and that is why their study is so important for the study of social and economic history. The group of fourteen historians whose essays are collected here therefore deserve our attention and respect for reviving a once-flourishing field of research and debate. As Reinhold Reith notes in his contribution, participants in Germany alone included names like Lujo Brentano, Gustav Schmoller, Werner Sombart and Otto von Zwiedineck-Søndenhorst, while British contributions include the Webbs' *Industrial Democracy* (1897) and G.D.H. Cole's *The Payment of Wages* (1918).

Though less fashionable in recent years, the study of the history of wage forms is also crucial for understanding the profound changes in labour relations we are experiencing today. The growing importance of social security in comparison to wage levels, as apparent for instance in recent demonstrations about pensions, as well as the international debate about legal minimum wages indicate a new stage in the development of wage labour. If we were able to put this transformation into a wider historical context we might perhaps be able to distinguish better between state administered pay-as-you-go pension schemes and those 'second pillar' funds or 'third pillar' individual savings, between piece rates and time rates, between different regimes of pay differentials and between individual and collective wages and salaries, profit-sharing and share ownership, etc.

In these respects *Experiencing Wages* is a breakthrough in social and economic history and the editors in their introduction rightly pay tribute to what has been achieved in this attempt to resume and carry forward the study of wage forms. But equally the collection cannot disguise the fact that the debate remains largely isolated, fragmented and discontinuous. Even within the collection, the individual essays do not relate to each other and lack a common background and focus. Three of the ten are not even strictly relevant to the subject: those of Harald Deceulaer on guild privileges in Antwerp, Patricia Van den Eeckhout on terms of notice, and Jane Humphries on child labour. One gets the impression that, despite the special colloquium at which they were presented, each author follows her or his own agenda packed in a special terminology. Even the central term, 'wage form', is used with different meanings: Henny Gooren and Hans Heger as well as Reinhold Reith use it as a category to distinguish remuneration by money from remuneration in kind, rights, entitlements, etc., as opposed to 'wage systems' denoting wages based on piece versus time rates, wage differentials or participation in ownership and profits, which other authors subsume under wage forms. In a strict sense under this definition of 'wage form' the sub-title of the book is incorrect with regard to most contributions. Conversely, the terms 'work' and 'labour' often seem to be used synonymously such as in the editors' introduction: 'people often combined and alternated wage labour with other forms of work and income' (p.7). Isn't work the result of labour? The editors assert, 'The main issue of this volume is that of *payment* for specific work' (p.7). Do the editors not mean 'payment of labour' as distinct from the sale of work by the craftsman? But such critical questions are perhaps out of place as the contributions do not complement each other in any consistent way.

This isolation exists also with regard to other related work. Important publications that are either ignored or remain marginal include Richard Biernacki's *The Fabrication of Labor: Germany and Britain, 1640–1941* (1995), Bernard Friot's *Puissances du salariat, emploi et protection sociale à la française* (1997) and Robert Castel's *Les metamorphoses de la question sociale, une chronique du salariat* (1995). Debates such as that on 'Free and Unfree Labour' at the International Institute of Social History in Amsterdam (1995), the international 'Labour Process Debate' with their publications and annual conferences, the discussion on 'The Dynamics of Wage Relations in the New Europe' in Maastricht (1997) do not appear on the horizon. This absence only reflects a general malaise shared to various degrees by all these 'debates' imprisoned in their separate academic disciplines, journals and conferences.

Some authors of *Experiencing Wages*—Michael Huberman, Skari Heikkinen Lina Gúlves-Munos and Paul Johnson—try to explain what determines different wage forms, for example strict economic rationality (according to human capital theory) or customs. Craig Muldrew and Steven King explore the impact of the shortage of currency on the early development of wage labour (pp.155–79). However, narrative and empirical evidence prevail and in fact represent the book's strength. I found most interesting the contributions on profit-sharing in Lancashire 1870–1914 by Huberman, on labour disputes in Germany during the eighteenth and early nineteenth centuries by Reinhold Reith, and on the endemic shortage of coined money and the many forms of remuneration of labour in England 1650–1800 by Muldrew and King. Almost all of the contributions present extensive original empirical research on relevant subjects.

Pieter Scholliers and Leonard Schwartz do not pretend that their introduction provides a coherent discussion of the issue, but any reader interested

in the development of wage labour will find interesting material in a collection that can be recommended without reservation. Perhaps it goes
without saying that marxists will be disappointed that no attempt is made
to relate the development of wage labour to capital accumulation and class
antagonism.

Scholliers and Schwarz 'firmly believe that the history of wage awaits a
bright and shining future'. I wish I could share their belief.

Jörn Janssen

Joe England, *The Wales TUC 1974–2004: Devolution and Industrial Politics*
(University of Wales Press, Cardiff, 2004), ISBN 0–7083–1919–X, xiv +136
pp., £12.99 pbk.

Joe England's book is a welcome addition to a Welsh labour history that has
mainly focused on studies of the late nineteenth century through to the
Second World War. This study of the Wales TUC marks a significant advance
in charting the development of the Welsh labour movement in the second
half of the twentieth century.

The Wales TUC emerged in the context of rising devolutionary pressures
in the 1960s. The initial moves were orchestrated by the Transport and
General Workers' Union (TGWU) within Wales as a reaction to rising unemployment in industrial areas. There had been earlier calls for an organisation
along the lines of the Scottish TUC by nationalists and communists but this
was rejected, primarily by trade union-leaders in north-east Wales who felt
that their economic and political interests were more closely bound with
north-west England. This was reflected in the existence of two TUC
Regional Advisory Committees, one for the north and one for the south. In
1969 the two bodies agreed to meet regularly and sowed the seeds of one
organisation that would cover the whole of Wales.

As a precursor to the Wales TUC, the TGWU amalgamated its two Welsh
regions (4 and 13) to create one body in 1968. Within the TGWU, Tom Jones
from north Wales and George Wright, an Englishman, are seen as crucial in
pushing the project for a Wales TUC forward. Jones became the first all-
Wales secretary of the TGWU in 1968 and was followed by Wright in 1972.
The appointment of Jones was crucial in winning over sceptics in the moderate north to a policy of amalgamation.

After some persuasion and negotiation within respective unions and the
TUC, the Wales TUC was established in 1974, replacing the Regional
Advisory Committees. England charts the negotiations in great detail, but
does so through a biographical survey of some of the protagonists. The

Wales TUC was at the forefront of campaigning against job losses in the coal and steel industries during the 1970s. However, it depended on the TGWU for staff and finances, with some in the Welsh labour movement viewing it as an adjunct of the larger organisation. Unemployment started to rise from 1976 onwards across north Wales with the closure of Courtaulds in Flint in 1977 and the end of steel making at Shotton in 1980. In the south, National Coal Board officials voiced concern at the impact that steel closures could have on the coal industry. The Wales TUC responded with calls for industrial action to defend jobs corresponding with the steel strike of 1980. This led to moves by the South Wales NUM to tie job losses in steel to pit closures. Miners' leaders, Emlyn Williams and George Rees, felt that the Wales TUC could be the main co-ordinating body of such action. This led to a fractious period between the TUC and the Wales TUC, with the former becoming increasingly critical of the latter's militant stance.

The autonomous action of the Wales TUC was personified by its support of the South Wales NUM's call for a national coal strike against pit closures in January 1980. A year later the Conservative government withdrew its closure programme in response to miners in south Wales coming out on unofficial strike.

The defeat of the miners in 1985 ushered in the wilderness years of the Wales TUC. Yet as England points out, the organisation made significant headway in its relationship with successive Conservative Secretaries of State for Wales. Peter Walker and David Hunt were willing to meet with the Wales TUC, but John Redwood and William Hague proved less willing to consult. Within this context the organisation took a more pragmatic approach to the reality of the new industrial relations culture. Throughout the 1980s and 1990s it was criticised from the left for promoting single union deals, no-strike agreements and inward investment at any price. England is sympathetic to its role, seeing it as a pragmatic response to de-industrialisation and high unemployment. Moreover, such pragmatism ensured union survival in a hegemonic culture that was persuading employers to pursue a policy of de-recognition. With the election of a Labour government in 1997 the Wales TUC welcomed a positive future and the realisation of its long-held policy of devolution.

England stresses that his study of the Wales TUC tackles the problem of an over-concentration on strikes, class struggle and militancy. This is true, but it also fails to address some other problems within Welsh labour historiography; most notably the relationship between the industrial south and the north east. The book tends to overemphasise the support for the organisation across Wales. England accepts that the trade union movement in north east Wales was initially sceptical, but fails to acknowledge the fact that the divisions between north and south remained through to the 1990s. In 1974, Ted McKay, the leader of the North Wales NUM, reported to his executive that the Wales TUC was dominated by the south. In 1978 he challenged the fact that the South Wales NUM had two seats on the general council and the north had none. In 1980–1 the North Wales Miners' Executive refused to support industrial action over closures, with McKay branding pickets from south Wales as 'bully boys' and 'yobbos'. This fractious relationship within Wales would have disastrous repercussions in the miners' strike of 1984–5, but these tensions remain absent from the text.

There is also a tendency to blame the defeat of the miners in 1985 on the leadership of Scargill. Along with other Welsh historians, England attempts to re-write history and absolve the South Wales NUM from the policy of industrial action against pit closures without a national ballot. He acknowledges that in 1980 the south Wales leadership had criticised the NUM executive for not sanctioning strike action, with Emlyn Williams stating that 'when it comes to catastrophic effects on unemployment to hell with the constitution' (p.50). The South Wales miners subsequently rejected strike action in a pit head ballot. Yet in the chapter on the miners' strike of 1984–5 he claims that 'divisions within the NUM created by the failure to hold a national ballot on strike action, combined with the reckless tactics of the national leadership, alienated members of other unions' (p.62). Such an argument could equally be mounted against the actions of Williams and Rees four years earlier.

However, these are minor criticisms of a detailed, methodical, and passionate study of the role played by the Wales TUC within a de-industrialising British economy. On its thirtieth anniversary in 2004, David Jenkins as its retiring general secretary reflected that 'despite the Dark Ages for trade unionism from 1979 to 1997 we kept the flag flying in Wales' (p.118). England's book is a fitting celebration of that achievement.

Keith Gildart
University of Wolverhampton

Francis Beckett, *Stalin's British Victims* (Sutton Publishing, Stroud, 2004), ISBN 0–7509–32223–6, xi+209pp., £20 pbk.

There will be few readers of this journal who are not acquainted with the previous works of Francis Beckett. In particular, his early work in the Soviet archives, culminating in his 1995 book *Enemy Within—The Rise and Fall of British Communism* was a trail-blazing work which, if it did not always satisfy purists, did at least demonstrate to a wider world the extent of the revelations that the Moscow archives held for historians of the Communist Party of Great Britain (CPGB). Since the publication of that book, Beckett has written a biography of Clement Attlee, and a moving and sensitive account of the life of his own father, the one-time Labour and ILP MP, and subsequent fascist, John Beckett. In this latest volume, however, Francis Beckett returns to the milieu of British and international communist politics between the wars.

The result is a rather curious volume. The 'victims' identified are in fact four British women: Rose Cohen, Rosa Rust, Freda Utley, and Pearl Rimel. Cohen was a British communist considered a beauty by many who knew her; Harry Pollitt famously proposed to her on no fewer than fourteen occasions before she married Max Petrovsky. Petrovsky was the Comintern representative to the British and French Communist Parties in the mid-1920s; when his spell of residence in the west ended he returned to Russia, accompanied by his wife. In 1937, at the height of the Soviet terror, he was arrested, and he was subsequently executed. Cohen herself was arrested later in the same year, and shot as a British spy.

Freda Utley, for her part, was a very intelligent woman starting on an academic career when she met and fell in love with a Russian, Arcadi Berdichevsky. Never quite as orthodox a communist as Cohen, Utley was nonetheless a socialist who was favourable towards the Soviet experiment in the 1920s, and after their marriage in 1928 they too went to live in the USSR. Berdichevsky was arrested in 1936, and Utley never saw him again: he was shot, and she ended up living in the United States, where she became a right-wing critic of communism. After publishing numerous books, including her important autobiography, *Lost Illusion* (1949), she died in 1978.

Rosa Rust was the daughter of the leading British communist, Bill Rust, and his first wife, Kay. Born in London, she moved with her parents to Moscow in 1928 and, at the age of three, literally forgot how to speak English after a serious illness. The collapse of her parents' marriage—Beckett provides a compelling view of Rust as a 'sexual predator' (p.8)—ended, rather oddly, with Bill returning to Britain with a new Russian partner, Tamara Kravets, while Kay and Rosa remained in Russia. In 1937, Kay's new husband, Misha, was arrested and shot. It was made clear to Kay that she must leave the country, but at the same time that she would not be allowed to take Rosa, now entering her teens, with he—Beckett surmises that this was effectively a way in which the Russians could keep a hold over Rust. Rosa was in Moscow in 1940 and 1941, but was then forced to leave the capital. Moving to the south of Russia, she ended up in the Volga German

Republic at just the point when its inhabitants were being deported to Kazakhstan, and, in the confusion, she could not avoid sharing their fate. It was only thanks to Georgi Dimitrov, the head of the Comintern, that she was finally able to leave Kazakhstan, to return to Russia before sailing from Murmansk to Leith, where she was put on a train for London, finally being reunited with her parents at Euston station. It was an awkward reunion, and the CPGB felt the full force of the awkwardness. Rosa was something of an embarrassment for both the party and for Bill Rust himself. This was never more so than at Rust's funeral in 1950, when it was initially intended by the party that she and her mother would not attend, and it was only thanks to a late intervention by Harry Pollitt that they were allowed to take a prominent role in the ceremony. Perhaps unsurprisingly, she never joined the Communist Party. In many ways, Beckett is at his liveliest when writing about Rust, perhaps because hers is in some ways the best and freshest story of the four, but also because he met her and formed a very favourable impression of her before her death in Redcar in April 2000, aged 74.

The final member of Beckett's quartet is Pearl Rimel. Like the others, a Londoner, she was a Jew born in 1912, who fell in love with, and in 1931 married, a Dutch Jew, George Fles. Fles moved to Moscow in 1932; she followed him in 1933. They moved to Tbilisi in 1935, but the following year Fles was arrested, and Pearl never saw him again. In this case, Beckett builds on the extensive research done by Fles's great-nephew, Thijs Berman, to describe the dismal life that Fles lived in prison before dying in a camp near Smolensk in 1939. Pearl returned to Britain, and died in 1983. It is interesting, to say the least, that her sisters and their husbands did not accept that the Soviets had done anything wrong, and remained members of the CPGB until its demise in 1991.

This brief summary does not really do justice to the depth and nuance that there is in this book. It is in many ways an excellent volume, which does a great deal to give tangible reality to what can so easily become the bald statistics of the Soviet Terror. Beckett's great strength is his ability to animate his subjects, and to show us what was happening through their eyes. If aspects of the narrative seemed rather familiar—the story of Andrew Rothstein in a Soviet prison cell, which appeared more than once in *Enemy Within*, needed no retelling here, while William Campbell's exploits as Villi the Clown are also well known by now—the book was cleverly conceived, and it is a very good read.

There are some criticisms, of course. The first, in a sense, relates to the book's title. The only 'British victim' (in the sense of losing her own life) described here is Cohen. Her story, however, is the best known of all the ones here. It is true that Beckett adds some useful detail, in part as a result of his use of the papers of, and interviews with, Cohen's niece, Joyce Rathbone. Cohen emerges from the book less sympathetically than I would have expected—it is hard to read Beckett and not come away with the view that she was rather manipulative, and something of a snob and social climber, whose affection for Petrovksy was based in part at least on *what* he was, as well as *who* he was. Cohen was no political innocent: she had been around far left politics for many years, and, while she could not have been expected to have anticipated anything as awful as the 1930s Soviet terror when she left for Moscow, she was not so naïve as to be unaware of the severe and serial abuses of human rights that had begun virtually from the moment that the Bolsheviks had taken power in 1917. Indeed, she had gloried in them: they were part of the construction of socialism under Lenin as well as under his successors. None of this meant that Cohen deserved her fate. But it does mean that she deserves to be treated 'warts and all'—something Beckett mostly achieves—rather than as some kind of plaster saint, which she assuredly was not.

Beckett also questions whether Cohen ever renounced her British citizenship, and, on the assumption that she did not, has some strong words for the British Foreign Office's failure to do more to try to save her. This is an important point in itself. But it has a further significance. If it is true that Cohen had a British passport but was nonetheless left to her fate, then previous assumptions that British communist leaders were relatively secure from the terror—because they would ultimately be able to rely on Foreign Office protection—carry less weight than has previously been thought. In this context, the talk of a Comintern show trial in 1937, with Pollitt as one of the key defendants, becomes more plausible still. However, the fact that Beckett is mainly filling in the gaps in the one case where the 'victim' was actually done to death by the Soviets gives a certain sense of disappointment overall. He makes a strong case for seeing the other three as 'victims', which of course they were, but at the side of the millions who actually died it might be argued that their suffering, although shocking, was essentially peripheral to the terror itself.

A second criticism is that, at times, the book's structure was a little confusing. While one can understand Beckett's desire to avoid a straightforward four-way split, in places the structure did seem unnecessarily fussy—this is not a book that offers up its information all that easily, even with the help of the index. And, despite Beckett's protestations that he does not want to be seen as an academic, it really is time that he started to include footnotes in his works, simply to ensure that they are taken as seriously as they deserve to be by academic audiences.

Is there any more to be said on this subject? Not on Cohen, perhaps. But during the 1920s, a small but steady stream of British communists applied, successfully, to have their party membership transferred from the British to the Soviet Communist Party, because they were going, with their families, to start a new life in what they saw as 'the workers' state'. Many of their names are contained in the minutes of CPGB committees. What would be really fascinating would be to try to find out what happened to *them*, in the 1930s and, assuming that any of them survived, thereafter. Perhaps they returned to Britain, chastened and anti-communist, like Freda Utley and Pearl Rimel. Perhaps they were killed, like Rose Cohen. Or perhaps they ended up in a maelstrom of confusion, like Rosa Rust. This book may be the last word about its four subjects, but it is to be hoped that it will inspire some ambitious and enterprising scholar to try to find out what happened to others, and whether any of them fell victim to the horrors that attended Soviet communism in the 1930s.

Andrew Thorpe
University of Exeter

Ed Cray, *Ramblin' Man: The Life and Times of Woody Guthrie* (W.W. Norton, New York and London, 2004) ISBN 0-393-04759-8, xxiii+488pp., $29.95 / £17.50 hbk.

Joe Klein's *Woody Guthrie: A Life* (1980) has long been the standard biography of America's foremost itinerant songster. Widely recognised as a landmark in biographical writing, Klein's book has never been out of print. Klein's fellow journalist Ed Cray has now written a new biography. *Ramblin' Man: The Life and Times of Woody Guthrie* has a difficult act to follow, but retells the story with help from some 10,000 items in the recently opened Woody Guthrie Archives.

Woodrow Wilson Guthrie was born in Okemah, Oklahoma in 1912, the son of Nora and Charley Guthrie. From Nora Guthrie, Woody inherited a repertoire of Anglo-Irish ballads, late nineteenth-century sentimental songs and his musical ability. From Charley Guthrie came Woody's intellectual curiosity and public spirit, though Woody's politics would diverge from his father's virulent anti-socialism. Guthrie's childhood was one of economic hardship and emotional trauma. Charley was a real estate speculator whose fortunes rocketed and crashed with the Oklahoma oil boom. Nora suffered from Huntington's Disease, a rare neurogenetic disorder that led to increasingly volatile behaviour and eventually, to tragedy. Fires would recur through

Guthrie's life like symbolism in a bad novel: Guthrie's parents lost their first home in a fire, his sister Clara died in a house fire, and in 1927 Guthrie's father was badly burned in a third fire, probably started by Nora. As a result, Charley was laid up for eighteen months recovering from burns and Nora was admitted to the Central State Hospital for the Insane. Aged fifteen, Guthrie's itchy-footed lifestyle began. Whereas his brothers and sister would settle down into the respectable conformity espoused by their father, Guthrie's restlessness would last until the mid 1950s, when he too was hospitalised by the hereditary Huntington's.

Cray's book expertly plots the childhood, the turbulent love life, the gradual onset of Huntington's Disease, the harrowing death by attrition and the intervening thirty years in which Guthrie became a living folk legend for his own generation and a lodestone of integrity for the next. Guthrie wrote literally thousands of songs, hundreds of newspaper columns, a fictionalised autobiography and an autobiographical novel. Though Guthrie played fast and loose with basic facts, his own life story provided most of the raw material he needed. He performed in countless concerts, benefits and fundraisers; he made scores of radio programmes and records. Highlights included his 1940 album of *Dustbowl Ballads* and the explosive creativity of his month spent on the payroll of the Bonneville Power Administration in 1941. Commissioned to write songs about the building of the Grand Coulee Dam, he produced twenty-six over a three-week period, including 'Pastures of Plenty' and 'Roll on, Columbia'. At the height of his powers, the carefully honed lyricism of his songs drew upon the past—he borrowed most of his tunes from elsewhere—and gave the chaos of contemporary history the structure and significance of myth.

Ed Cray's research into Guthrie's life and unorthodox career is exhaustive. The wayward eighteen-year-old Guthrie struck up a friendship with a Mrs Todd, employee of Pampa Public Library; Cray tracks down an interview with her. Guthrie was the subject of a bulging FBI file; Cray quotes this sometimes comically inaccurate version of Guthrie's story. Cray's book is also full of the voices of Guthrie's family and friends, over seventy of whom he interviewed for the book.

Guthrie's considerable charisma sometimes tipped into messianic self-belief; the biggest challenge faced by his biographer is to resist the pull of Guthrie's own self-engrossed magnetism. 'I've wrote a million pages and I've never read a one' Guthrie once claimed, a phrase that encapsulates the central paradox. Guthrie was a self-educated intellectual who pushed his erudition into the background in order to have his authenticity on display. He needed intellectual and cultural resources—musical, literary, political and artistic traditions—to give voice to the experiences he'd shared with the dust-bowl refugees he called his people. But allowing his learning to show would, he thought, damage credibility. He eagerly read Steinbeck's novel *The Grapes of Wrath*, later pretending that he'd only seen the film; he was a far better musician and singer than he let on; behind closed doors he enjoyed the modernist compositions of John Cage. Many of Guthrie's friends and colleagues point out these contradictions and Cray himself often draws attention to Guthrie's self-styled primitivism, but elsewhere the book succumbs to the romance. In one short chapter dealing with Guthrie's freight-car trip to California in 1937 for example, Cray capitulates to Guthrie's self-mythology and, in the absence of any other evidence, reproduces the content and tone of Guthrie's highly artful autobiography as biographical fact.

Guthrie was a political artist entangled in history. In places, Cray's feel for political and historical context potently infuses his account of Guthrie's writing. So the passages on the post-war period subtly chart the dissolution of Guthrie's Popular Front world: as the political optimism of the New Deal period gave way to the edgy conservatism of the Cold War, Guthrie and his circle quickly started to seem like anachronistic figures. Woody's work suffered and the powerful late 1930s writing yielded to brittle slogans and hints of nostalgia. But sometimes Cray's account lacks such nuance and in particular he never gets to the bottom of Guthrie's long and complex relationship with the Communist Party. Guthrie became close to the CP in the mid 1930s, wrote 280 columns for its publications and described himself as a Marxist (though he preferred 'Marxican'). Cray caricatures the Communist Party as a nest of manipulative and stiff-necked Stalinists. If this is all it ever was, Guthrie's longstanding affiliation makes little sense. But even though Cray is better on Guthrie's life than his times, this book represents a significant achievement and a major contribution to research on one of the most important American political writers of the last century

Ben Harker
University of York

Moshe Lewin, *The Soviet Century* (Verso, London, 2005), ISBN 1–84467–016–3, 352pp., £25 hbk.

Readers will remember Lewin as the author of *Lenin's Last Struggle* which drew on documentary evidence to demonstrate Lenin's opposition to the growing power of Stalin, just before the former's death in January 1924. This was taken to vindicate Trotsky's version of the succession. With this volume Lewin begins the quest for an understanding of the Soviet Union, drawing on the wealth of new materials available to post-communist historians. His introduction makes clear that he sees this job as handicapped from the start by the legacy of the Cold War. In particular he points to the 'public discourse' which it manufactured about the USSR 'based on deeply ingrained but unverified assumptions' and 'the unilateral focus on misdeeds and crimes characteristic of propaganda', which in Lewin's view 'ludicrously inflated, impossible, and quite unverifiable number[s] of [Stalin's] victims'. Lewin discusses the fact that millions died in the USSR's short history but doesn't make the explicit connection between that fact and the persuasiveness of the public discourse he refers to. What is offered here, to cause us to rethink the Soviet past, is not a history of the USSR but a three-part investigation covering 'the Stalinist period', 'the post-Stalinist period' and finally a third part which broaches the 'Soviet era' as a whole. Let us look at each of these in turn.

The story of Stalin's rise to power focuses on his 'profoundly authoritarian personality' and his capacity to gather 'around himself an expanding group of insignificant acolytes and sycophants like Voroshilov or Budenny'. Stalin, we are told, was a parochial figure untouched by the cultures of the second or third Internationals. Lewin allows that in this sense he was representative of one of the two 'political and cultural universes' which coexisted in the Bolshevik Party until the end of the civil war. He also allows that 'dictatorship was the only available option' at this stage of Soviet history (p.14). But more than one type of dictatorship was possible and whereas Lenin (and Trotsky, Rakovsky, etc.) came to the view, according to Lewin, that federalism was necessary to address the nationalities question, Stalin and his supporters were firm centralisers. Their 'clear and simple vision' prevailed after Lenin's death and Trotsky's fateful equivocation in the spring of 1924. Stalin's philosophy—expressed in the conviction that with good cadres nothing is impossible, (on the assumption of an all-powerful state)—took the form of an extreme voluntarism with deadly characteristics. It encompassed a militaristic perspective born of the civil war and entailed the transformation of the party into an instrument for controlling the state. Stalin used his position as general secretary to render this 'master plan' (p.38) real and in so doing destroyed the Bolshevik Party, picking off the opposition one faction at a time. So far this is a familiar tale, developed over the years by those keen to emphasise the rupture between Lenin and Stalin and their respective theories and practices. Lewin's rendition occasionally wavers from this path; the party which he tells us Stalin destroyed in the 1930s is still (somewhat confusingly) threatened with extinction 'as a ruling institution' in 1946 (p.136).

He provides new evidence showing that between 1922 and 1935 about 1.5 million members left the party, a huge pool, as he puts it, of self-declared 'enemies of the people' who were targets for the NKVD during the purges. He also argues that new evidence shows that 'Stalin had the first and last word on everything' after the consolidation of his personal dictatorship. This was a system of micro-management to an extraordinary and dysfunctional extent, especially after the first Five-Year Plan was launched. 'Unparalleled violence' accompanied the massive experiment in social engineering unleashed in both town and country as the dictatorship waged war on the peasantry in the 1930s. As late as 1939, 67 per cent of the population still lived in the countryside, even though the urban population had doubled since 1927. The influx of peasants to the towns in these twelve years had assumed 'gigantic proportions' and Lewin emphasises the prevalence of rural origins in the urban population throughout the inter-war years. To the 640 towns inherited from Tsarist Russia, 450 were added between 1927 and 1939. Such figures disguise the fact, as Lewin points out, that 'masses of people' also abandoned the towns in the same period, as workers sought more food and refuge from physical and nervous exhaustion. Rates of population growth—up by a million per year between 1923 and 1928 (under NEP)—fell under these circumstances between 1928 and 1940. 1933 actually saw a negative demographic balance.

Collectivisation was an economic as well as a social and political disaster. Without food grown in the peasants' 'household plots' the whole country would have starved. Yet to introduce collectivism a massive coercive machine was constructed to compel the bulk of the population to do something—work the land—they had once done voluntarily. Peasants fled to the towns, while the regime tried to restore order with internal passports and other coercive devices. This social flux and volatility—an aspect of Soviet experience missing from accounts of totalitarianism which focus exclusively on the state apparatus—is also visible in evidence of hundreds of strikes (involving party members) in the NEP period, and in open and clandestine opposition in the 1930s (including opposition by suicide). The man who was more responsible than anyone else for the 'social magma' which threatened to run out of control—Stalin—grew stronger, according to Lewin, because 'the top echelon', 'overwhelmed by problems and undermined by doubts' turned to him as the one person who was sufficiently tough and determined to stem the flow (p.82).

Stalin in any case emasculated 'all institutions of any weight', including the politburo itself. The apparatus, meanwhile, became ever more complex. The politburo, the orgburo, the secretariat and, above all, Stalin 'immersed themselves in local minutiae' (p.89) and attempted to micromanage a continent from Moscow. The general secretary would not delegate powers downwards. But he did find mistakes everywhere and normally interpreted them as faults to be punished. His labours 'assumed pathological proportions' as 'he aimed at personal mastery of a complex totality that no one had ever mastered', including a constant meddling in the arts, the sciences, the military, and so on (p.90). The purges of 1937–8 provided him 'with a new historical alibi'. Lewin argues that the documentary evidence shows that few people knew what was happening even within the political elite (p.104). Certainly few could imagine the mechanics and scope of the slaughter. Pospelov, set up to investigate the period by Khrushchev in 1955, reported that 1,548,366 persons were arrested for anti-Soviet activities, of whom 681,692 were shot. These were party members and state cadres; Pospelov said nothing of the enormous numbers of 'socially alien elements' who also fell under the axe. Lewin puts the total arrested in the years 1930–53 at 3,778,000, of whom 786,000 were executed (p.106). He also puts the pre-war camp population at a peak of 1,979,729, again drawing on Russian sources published since 1991. This figure includes common criminals. Lewin seems content with his idea that 'the state's terrorist machinery and activity remained veiled in secrecy, even from otherwise well-informed top officials' (p.111). Obviously the size of the country, the remoteness of the camps and the fear of punishment helped in this achievement. But he doesn't ask—as students of the Nazi terror have been forced to ask—how many people were required to administer this system from the stage of mass arrests to the administration of railways, camps, forced labour factories/canals/cities and other gigantic enterprises, including the forced removal of whole populations and the executions of at least three quarters of a million people. He tells us that hundreds of thousands of common criminals were released after Beria took over from Yezhov in November 1938. Did they never speak of their experiences? What about the hundreds of thousands who were released during the war, to fight the Nazis? Could the truth be contained in their heads alone and those of the ruling circle? Many NKVD officials were themselves punished for breaches of discipline —Lewin tells us that documents prove this. Was there no leakage of information from this unreliable element?

By 1953 the monstrous, inefficient, irrational, beast of the Gulag was ripe for dismantling (p.122). At Stalin's death the camp population included 600,000 political prisoners, out of a total exceeding three million—or five million ('an all-time record') if we include those exiled and imprisoned (p.154). Lewin thinks that in total around four million people were sentenced for political crimes in the years 1920–53; twenty per cent of them were shot, the vast majority of these after 1930. Some estimates cited here suggest that about 1.6 million inmates, including common-law prisoners, died in captivity between 1934 and 1953. In addition 1,800,000 'kulaks' were forcibly moved and about a half a million of these died in the process. Demographic losses for the period 1914–45—a period of wars, forced industrialisation, and famines as well as state terror—may be as high as seventy-four million (p.126). Though Lewin relies on R. W. Davies for this latter figure, he makes no mention of Robert Conquest, J. Arch Getty, or other disputants in the business of calculating Stalin's victims.

In the post-Stalin period political opposition continued to be repressed but the scale and brutality of repression decreased. To take one example; the number of 'counter-revolutionaries' fell from 580,000 in 1953 to 11,000 in 1959. By 1961 the percentage of common-law prisoners had increased from 10.7 per cent to 31.5 per cent of the total; the system of unpaid slave labour had been abolished, as had mass-exile settlements, once consisting of two million people. The powers of the secret police were gradually curtailed, the special courts were disbanded. Lewin acknowledges that it is not easy to know if the new rules were observed in practice (p.168) and he surmises that political prisoners generally had fewer rights than other inmates. But he assumes that the reforms created a distinct penal system compared with the one in force under Stalin. The secret police—who remained powerful enough to have a hand in the removal of Khrushchev in 1964—lost 'the outrageous power to judge and punish their victims themselves' (p.183). Despite the well-documented cases in which psychiatric wards were used to incarcerate people, Lewin argues that this was a regime which did not merit epithets such as 'Evil Empire'. It was a regime of 'laws, rights and gurantees' (p.199), compared with what had gone before.

A background factor here was the growing labour shortage and the growth of workers' rights—what Lewin calls the 'de-Stalinisation of the workplace'. Russia, the Ukraine and the Baltic states were majority urban populations by the mid–1960s subject to huge migratory movements; between 1961 and 1966, 29 million people moved to towns in the Russian Federation alone and 24.2 million left them (p.204). Much of this was spontaneous, while official attempts to induce labour to migrate to Siberia generally failed. Management of labour supply was a bureaucratic nightmare giving rise to anomalies such as towns with a dependence on predominantly male or predominantly female employment (p.212). Yet after Stalin's death the bureaucracy flourished as never before. Agencies proliferated, multiple sub-units with overlapping functions 'and myriad malfunctions' sprang into existence in search of answers. But below the summit, Kosygin noted, the bureaucracy wasn't doing very much and didn't care very much either.

Lewin shows that great progress was made in health care and education. He also details the perks of the rulers, which extended to a welfare state of 'luxurious proportions' (p.230). With the well-known exception of Brezhnev, politburo members were not much interested in luxury, but plenty of lesser functionaries were. Lewin devotes a couple of chapters to leaders such as Gromyko, Khrushchev, Kosygin and Andropov, but is adamant that the study of the Soviet Union has been held back by the traditional focus on leaders, actors, and ideology 'depicted as independent agents abstracted from their historical context'.

The Soviet Century is at its best when discussing the social transformations to which the system was subject and wants to rescue the Soviet era from 'the mendacious and nihilistic campaign' to which it has been subjected in Russia since 1991. The author sees Lenin as 'a political strategist par excellence, who was only reacting to what he perceived and understood of the crises he was living through' (p.272). The Bolshevik Revolution was expected to trigger revolution elsewhere and held out the prospect of social justice at home. It was not a socialist revolution; nor could it have been—the overwhelming majority of the population had not yet entered the industrial age. The country had already been plunged into 'indescribable chaos' before Lenin took power and the Bolsheviks were faced with full-blown civil war from July 1918—events which transformed the party to the point where the old Bolsheviks were unable to recognise it (p.290). Millions were killed, millions more died prematurely, millions were displaced, cities were denuded of their populations. As the West recovered from the war Russia was more backward than ever (p.297). This, for Lewin, is the social background for the rise of Stalinism, though he contends that the statist ideology that emerged in the ranks of the civil war combatants played its part too (p.291). Lewin talks about the right to free speech in Lenin's Bolshevik party, but says nothing about the extreme measures of centralisation which Lenin's party was forced to take to restore order. Nor does he discuss the ban on rival parties and the prohibition on party factions, to say nothing of the authoritarian doctrines to which Lenin himself subscribed. Surely all of this is relevant in explaining the rise of Stalin? What was left after Stalin's death, according to Lewin, was 'bureaucratic absolutism'—a system in which the party bosses had lost power to their bureaucrats (p.383). But it was also a society—in contrast to Russia in the 1990s—which valued culture, health, education, employment, and equality.

John Callaghan
University of Wolverhampton